Illustrated Transfer Techniques for Disabled People

Illustrated Transfer Techniques for Disabled People

Tony Pelosi

B App Sc (Phty) MCSP MAPA

Chief Physiotherapist, Mt Eliza Centre for Rehabilitation
and Extended Care, Melbourne, Australia

Margaret Gleeson

B App Sc (Phty) Grad.Dip.Ex.Rehab. MAPA

Physiotherapist, Multiple Sclerosis Society of Victoria,
Melbourne, Australia

FOREWORD BY

Peter L. Colville MB BS FACRM

Medical Director, National Multiple Sclerosis Society of Australia

Illustrated by Tony Harvey

CHURCHILL LIVINGSTONE
MELBOURNE EDINBURGH LONDON AND NEW YORK 1988

CHURCHILL LIVINGSTONE
Medical Division of Longman Group UK Limited

Distributed in Australia by Longman Cheshire Pty Limited,
Longman House, Kings Gardens, 95 Coventry Street,
South Melbourne 3205, and by associated companies,
branches and representatives throughout the world.

First published 1988

ISBN 0-443-03969-0

British Library Cataloguing in Publication Data
Pelosi, Tony
Illustrated transfer techniques for disabled people.
1. Physically handicapped
I. Title. II. Gleeson, Margaret
649.8   HV3011

Library of Congress Cataloging in Publication Data
Pelosi, Tony.
  Illustrated transfer techniques for disabled people.
  Bibliography: p.
  1. Transfer of sick and wounded—Pictorial works.
2. Sick—Positioning—Pictorial works. I. Gleeson,
Margaret. II. Title. [DNLM: 1. Handicapped.
2. Transportation—methods.   HV 3022 P392i]
RT87.T72P45 1988   616'.025   87–30020

Produced by Longman Publisher (Pte) Ltd.
Printed in Singapore

Foreword

A publication of this type represents an enormous investment in time to ensure that instructions and illustrations are clear, precise and correct. Both the authors have had much practical experience in performing and teaching transfer techniques and that expertise is obvious throughout this book.

Safe transfer techniques refer to the safety of both the person with disability who is transferring or being transferred, and the safety of those who assist. Injury to the assistant is much more common than injury to the disabled person.

Prevention of but a few such injuries would justify the total development cost of this publication, let alone justify the purchase of this copy.

In many situations requiring transfers there may be several satisfactory alternative methods. Skill in those alternatives will allow a best choice to be made. However where the individual has some limitation of problem-solving skills, has difficulty in motor planning or difficulty in learning or retaining new motor skills, learning too many alternatives may be counter productive and only generate confusion.

As with any manual of directions the reader is asked to study the illustrations carefully and 'if all else fails, read the instructions!'

Peter L. Colville

Preface

Many books have been written on the principles of safe lifting and transferring of people with disabilities. These often focus upon information about a specific disability type or, within a general approach, provide relatively small sections on actual transfer procedures. This manual provides procedures for a wide range of disability types and in many of the common transfer situations encountered by people with disabilities in their everyday lives. The transfers described are appropriate for the person in a hospital or a nursing home, as well as for those living at home and participating in the community.

There are many types of disabling conditions, such as arthritis, neurological disorders and common orthopaedic conditions, which can make movement difficult for a person. Often the person will need assistance to transfer from one place to another (for example, from a wheelchair to a car) and this can be done either with ease or with great difficulty for both parties. Even when the person does not require assistance, the change of position can be achieved well or poorly. Maximizing the efficiency and safety of such manoeuvres is of great benefit to the people with disabilities and their helpers, since many transfers are made during a day. The transfer and lifting techniques illustrated in this manual are designed to facilitate a wide range of everyday activities by suggesting procedures which are both safe and efficient.

The bulk of the manual is divided into chapters which represent the common transfer situations. Techniques requiring graded amounts of assistance are described in order to cater for individual capabilities. The best transfer technique is that which allows the individual with the disability to do as much of the transfer as is safely possible. By routinely incorporating these desirable procedures for transferring, the tendency for the person with the disability to become inappropriately dependent on others is reduced. In the long-term this enhances the quality of life of all involved. The person with the disability maintains optimal independence, whilst not unduly stressing the helper(s), and thus the probability of the person being able to remain in the community is improved.

It is strongly recommended that the person with a disability is assessed by a therapist in order to establish the best transfer techniques for the individual. A variety of techniques may be required for various daily activities of the person (for example during personal care, work and recreation). In this way appropriate variations on the transfer techniques described in this manual can be made to suit the requirements of each particular individual. These variations are made in accordance with the therapist's assessment of that person's specific needs. When established as the best for this individual, the transfers can be shown to and practised with the helper(s) who are usually involved in the care of the person. The helper may be a spouse, friend, attendant carer or a nurse.

It has been our experience that people with disabilities benefit from using consistent transfer techniques. Ideally, in a given situation the same procedure for changing position should be used each time. This can be difficult to achieve when there can be a number of different helpers involved with the person from time to time. As accessibility to a wide range of activities in the community improves, the person with a disability will be assisted by an increasing variety of helpers. Consequently it is hoped that information in this manual will assist in the training of a wide range of people. This may include health professionals, carers in the homes of people with disabilities, ambulance officers, taxi drivers and students, as well as people with disabilities. In this way, the desired consistency of transfer techniques will more likely be maintained amongst the helpers involved with the individual in a variety of settings.

As a general rule, if a helper is offering assistance for the first time, it is desirable to ask the person with a disability about the degree and type of assistance required and how the transfer is usually performed. The new helper is then not faced with assisting inappropriately or avoiding the contact altogether because of the unknown. Prior knowledge of a range of transfer and lifting techniques is an advantage if one is likely frequently to encounter people with disabilities needing assistance.

This manual also includes chapters on the management of spasticity and wheelchair management. Although these are not transfer or lifting techniques per se, capable management in these two areas can greatly assist the person for whom these are factors in their disability.

In conclusion, this manual does not contain an exhaustive list of lifting and transferring techniques but attempts to provide options for most common situations. Highly specialized techniques, such as team lifting of a spinally injured person, have not been included in this manual. Such strategies are generally the subject of specific training programmes in specialized units. Similarly this

manual is not an attempt to rewrite text books on
lifting, on spasticity or on equipment used by
people with disabilities.

The aim of this work is to demystify the handling of
people with disabilities and to preserve their dignity
and quality of life.

Melbourne 1988   Tony Pelosi
                              Margaret Gleeson

Acknowledgements

This book was developed from the recognition that there was a need. During its evolution we have filmed, edited, scrapped, written, rewritten, scrapped, drawn, redrawn, and scrapped many techniques before this, our best effort.

We thank everyone who helped us and in particular for their skills and forbearance the following people:

Filming — Barney and Jenny Gleeson, Joan Rowlands, Bob Thornton and Helen Watt;
Typing — Georgina Anderson, Bette Beynon and Keryn McNeill;

Illustrations — Tony Harvey;
Critique — Pat Baker, Dr Peter Colville and Dr Laurence Gleeson.

We especially acknowledge the generous support we have received from the Multiple Sclerosis Society of Victoria Limited and Australian Industrial Publications. Part of the proceeds from sales of this publication go to the Multiple Sclerosis Society of Victoria Limited.

This book is dedicated to those people and their families whose lives are made more difficult because of dependant disability.

Contents

PART ONE
Basic information

How to use this book

There are many situations in which people with disabilities need to change position. In this manual, common transfer situations are presented in separate chapters for easy reference. At the beginning of each chapter there is a list of all the transfer techniques and situations illustrated, along with a note of the degree of assistance needed and the number of helpers required to perform each transfer safely. This information is repeated on the top of the page illustrating that transfer technique. There is one technique to a page.

The degree of assistance needed is determined by the level of the person's ability and the classification is designed to allow maximal participation by the person with the disability.

As an example of how to use the book, let us assume a technique is needed to totally assist a person onto the toilet from a wheelchair.

Step 1 Turn to the table of contents and find the chapter 'Chair/toilet'.
Step 2 Turn to the list at the beginning of the chapter 'Chair/toilet' on page **65** and look for the pages of transfer techniques which are much assisted.
Step 3 Turn to the pages indicated in the list to find the appropriate technique which allows the transfer to be done safely.

Where it is important to the safety of the person transferring, reference is made to leading with the stronger side, or assisting on the weaker side. It is recognized that in the early stages of some neurological conditions, the rehabilitation goals of treatment will place different demands on the transfer techniques. The methods shown are those most appropriate to long-term management of transfer problems.

Safe lifting guidelines

The following checklist aims to protect people (both the lifters and the person with a disability) from injury during transfers.

1. Study the starting/finishing positions — particularly those of the feet — as illustrated in each transfer situation.
2. Make sure you can manage the transfer yourself. If not, seek assistance from another helper or use equipment if required.
3. General rules when lifting *anything*:
   - Have the weight (in this case a person with a disability) as close as possible to your body before lifting.
   - Take the strain by using your powerful leg muscles (Fig. 2.1A) rather than your back (Fig. 2.1B).
   - Brace stomach muscles prior to and during the lift so that your back is protected from injury.
   - Make sure you have a secure grip that is comfortable to you and the person you are lifting. Commonly used grips are illustrated on page 7.
   - If more than one helper is required for any technique, make sure the lift is co-ordinated so that both helpers lift at the same time. One helper should be designated to give the command: '1–2–3–lift', for example.
   - Tell the person what you plan to do before you do it, so that the person knows what is about to happen and can help you if possible. In this way you avoid undue strain.
   - Make sure you have enough clear space to perform the lift safely.
   - Suitable footwear is an important safety factor when lifting. Flat shoes are best.

This book shows how to assist people with a disability to transfer from place to place. In most instances movable equipment is involved, such as wheelchairs, beds and hoists. Make sure the equipment is stable before and during the lift. For example, put on the wheelchair's brakes.

The above points are not repeated throughout the book. It is essential that they are studied and understood if injury is to be avoided.

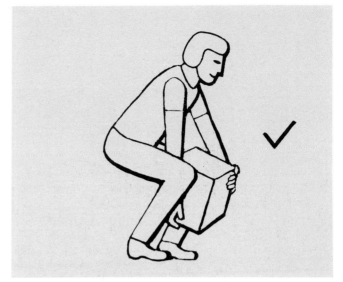

Fig. 2.1A Correct lifting technique uses leg muscles

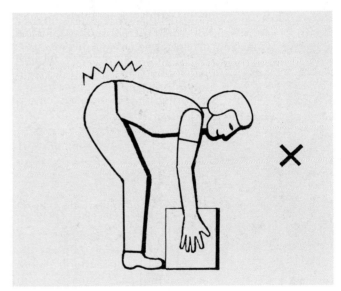

Fig. 2.1B Incorrect lifting technique risks back injury

Grips and accessories

GRIPS

A few commonly used grips are used throughout the text. For clarity they are shown here in more detail (see Fig. 3.1).

Points to note

- The grips should be firm and comfortable to the person and the helper(s).
- Decide on a grip before starting any transfer.
- The grips recommended are the most suitable for the techniques illustrated.

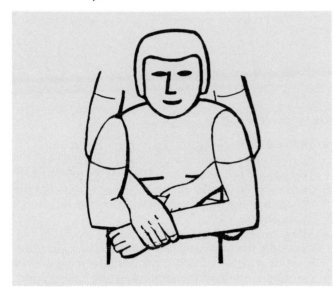

Fig. 3.1A Through-arm, wrist crossed-over grip

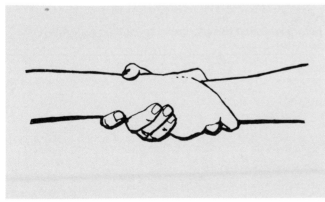

Fig. 3.1B Wrist grip

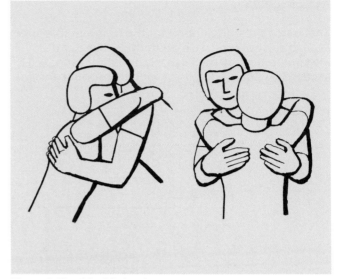

Fig. 3.1C Shoulder-blade grip

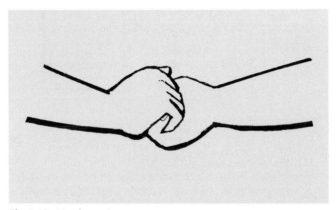

Fig. 3.1D Monkey grip

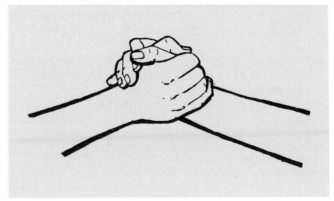

Fig. 3.1E Thumb-through grip

ACCESSORIES

This is not a resource book for the innumerable aids available for people with disabilities. Here, we attempt to portray the basic essentials of each accessory without details of specific product design.

Bath seat

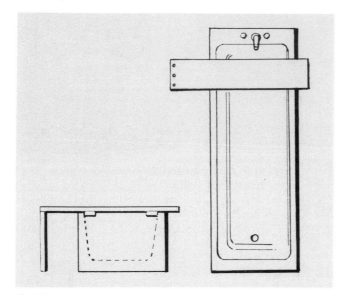

Fig. 3.2 Bath seat

- A bath seat (Fig. 3.2) is a frame, usually wooden, which forms a seat across a bath. The seat protrudes from the outside edge of the bath and is supported by an external leg. The leg is usually adjustable.
- The person transfers from a wheelchair first onto the protruding part of the seat. The person's legs are lifted over the edge of the bath and the person then moves across the seat to the centre of the bath.
- The person either remains seated over the bath to wash with a hand-held shower, or lowers down into the bath.

NOTE
Bath seats must be held securely onto the bath. This is usually achieved by two movable wooden cleats that fit snugly against the inside of the bath rims.

Mobile floor hoist

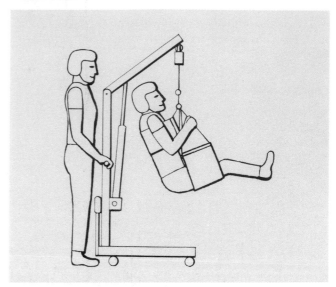

Fig. 3.3 Mobile floor hoist

- The mobile floor hoist (Fig. 3.3) is a hydraulic cranking device on castors which have brakes.
- The person is lifted by attaching slings to the hoist and cranking the handle to the appropriate height before transferring the person from one location to another.
- Many varieties of hoist and slings are available but generally the principles are similar. The key factor is safety. Effective brakes, proper attachments and careful planning of the movement are mandatory to the safe use of this equipment.

NOTE
Before your first use of a hoist, consult an experienced operator.

Rotating board

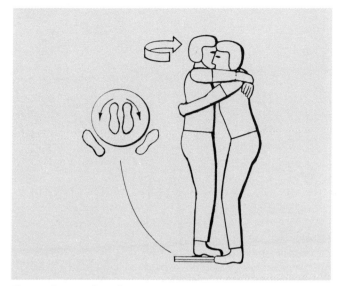

Fig. 3.4 Rotating board

- A rotating board (Fig. 3.4) consists of two discs, between which are ball-bearings to allow one disc to rotate on the other.
- The rotating board is used to help a person pivot on their feet when moving from one seat to another. The board is placed under the person's feet before standing. The helper stands with feet either side of the board and assists the person into standing on the middle of the board. The helper ensures that the person is balanced and that the feet do not slip.
- The person is then rotated by the helper to face in the new direction before sitting down again.

NOTE
Where the person's arm function permits, the rotating board can be used by the person unassisted.

Seat belt

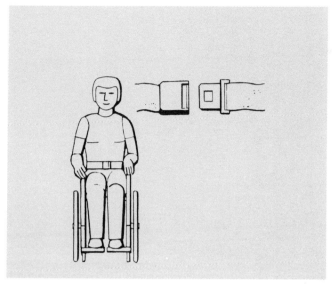

Fig. 3.5 Seat belt

- This belt (Fig. 3.5) is an adjustable continuous piece of webbing fastened in front with a conventional car seat belt safety buckle.
- The seat belt is used:
  — To give security to a person in a wheelchair or any other chair.
  — To assist a helper in moving a person. The seat belt is placed around the person's waist and the helper pulls on the belt during the move.

Grips and accessories

Bed stick

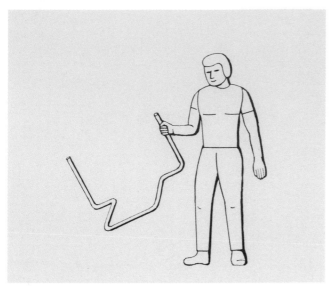

Fig. 3.6A Bed stick

- A bed stick (Fig. 3.6A) is a piece of tubular alloy with a smooth coat of non-corrosive material, and shaped as illustrated. It is placed under the mattress with the end sections protruding vertically as handles. The weight of the mattress holds it in place (Fig. 3.6B).

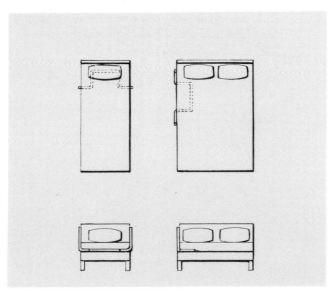

Fig. 3.6B Bed stick

- The bed stick is used by the person to assist movements within the bed (such as rolling over or moving towards the edge) or in sitting up or lying down. It can be used in a single or double bed.

Slide board

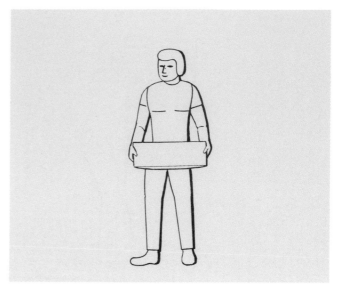

Fig. 3.7 Slide board

- A slide board (Fig. 3.7) is an oblong piece of timber designed to bridge the gap between two seats. It is highly polished to reduce friction.
- The board is placed between seats when the person is unable to take weight on their legs. The person uses the board to slide from seat to seat. It is preferable that the seats be of the same height. If one seat is hard or slippery (e.g. edge of bath or toilet) the board is safer when a small towel is folded and inserted between the board and the seat.

NOTE
Skin damage can result if care is not taken. It is preferable that the person be clothed when using a slide board, as this protects the skin and makes sliding easier.

Slide board mat

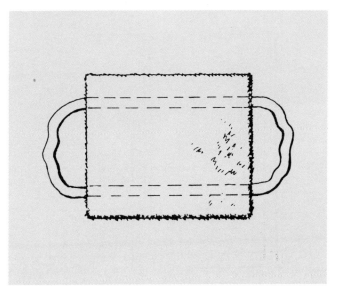

Fig. 3.8 Slide board mat

- A slide board mat (Fig. 3.8) is constructed from two squares of lambskin, sewn with the kid sides together. A rectangular loop of webbing is fastened between the squares by the stitching and protrudes to form handles on two opposite sides of the mat. The person sits on the mat which has been placed on top of a slide board.
- The helper moves the person across the slide board from seat to seat by pulling on one handle of the mat. This mat is very useful for heavy people or those with fragile skin.

Wheelchair straps

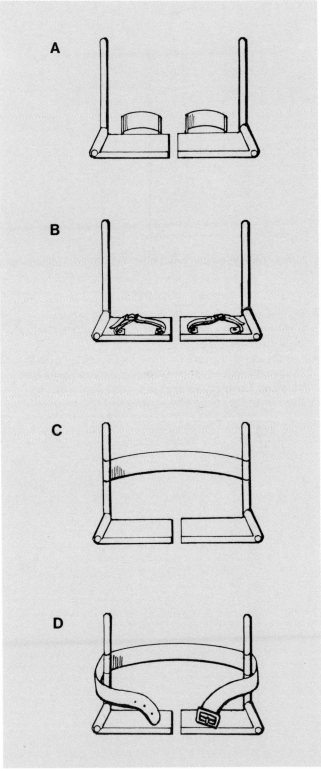

Fig. 3.9 Wheelchair straps: **A** heel straps; **B** toe straps; **C** calf strap; **D** shin strap

- Wheelchair straps (Fig. 3.9) are strips of fabric or leather which are attached to the wheelchair to keep the person's feet and/or legs in place.

Swimming pool mat

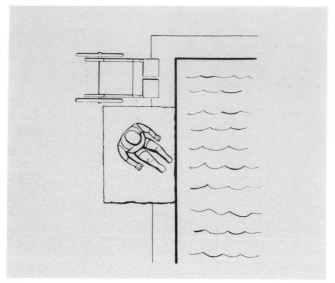

Fig. 3.10 Swimming pool mat

- A swimming pool mat (Fig. 3.10) is a large, light-weight piece of compressed rubber that can be rolled up for storage.
- Disabled swimmers use the mat to enter and leave the water where steps or hoists are not available. The mat protects swimmers from abrasions as they enter or leave the water over the pool side.

Monkey bar (ring bar)

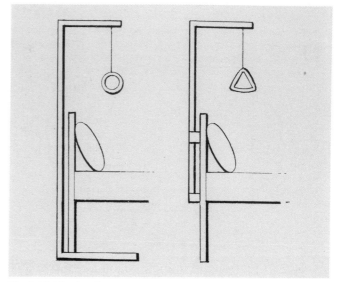

Fig. 3.11 Monkey bars

- A monkey bar (Fig. 3.11) is a handle suspended from a pole at the head end of a bed. The pole can be attached to the bed or to a free standing frame which sits on the floor behind the bed. The handles vary in shape but usually a ring or triangle is used.
- The monkey bar is used by a person in bed to move about or to transfer into a chair.

Blocks

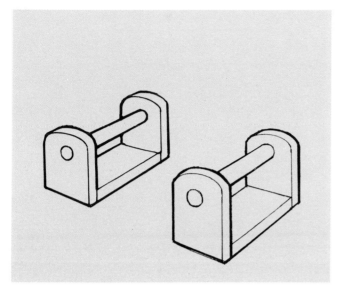

Fig. 3.12 Blocks

- A block (Fig. 3.12) is a raised handle on a firm base used by the person to raise the buttocks clear of the bed.
- A block can be improvised, using a few paperbacks tied firmly together.

Fixed overhead hoist

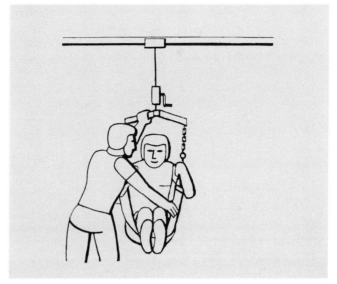

Fig. 3.13 Fixed overhead hoist

- A fixed overhead hoist (Fig. 3.13) utilizes a box door-track mounted on the ceiling at a point where transfers usually take place, such as toilet, bed or bath.
- A wheeled carriage with a hook is in the track. A means of hoisting the person is suspended from the hook. (Block and pulley system, mechanical crank or electrical crank.)
- Slings are positioned on the person and attached to the cranking device to effect the transfer.

PART TWO
Transfers and techniques

In bed movements

MUCH ASSISTED
Two helpers required

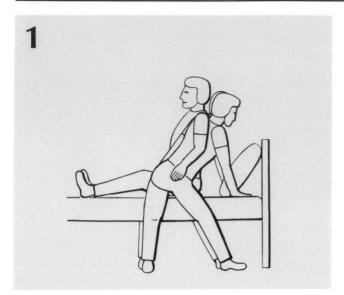

Helpers: Each put one hand behind person and press on bed. Put other hand beneath thighs of person and take a wrist grip with other helper. Make sure same foot as hand under thigh of person is pointing towards bed. Point other foot in line with the direction of the lift. Lean shoulder against person's chest below armpit.
Person: Put arms down the backs of helpers.

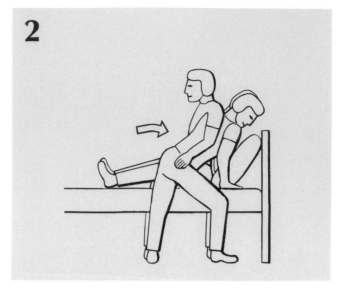

Helpers: Make sure head is between person and head of the bed. On command '1–2–3–lift', press hand on bed and shoulder against person and move person up or down bed.

NOTE
Helpers must lean firmly into the person's chest throughout the lift.

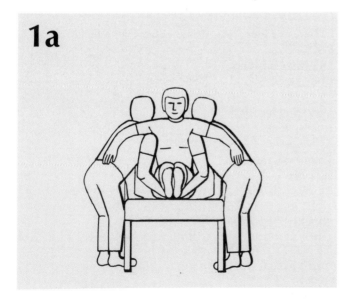

1

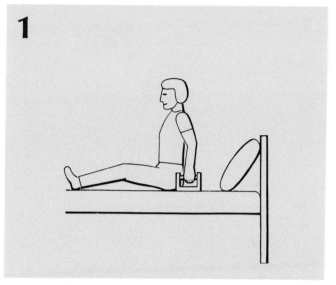

Sit up and place one block at each side just back from your hips, if moving up bed. If moving down, place blocks forward of hips.

2

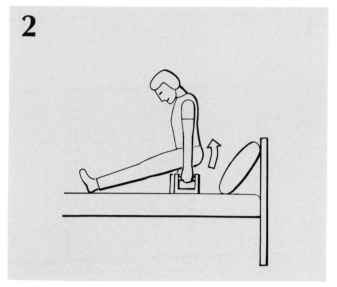

Push down with your hands and swing buttocks through and back to move up; forward to move down.

1a

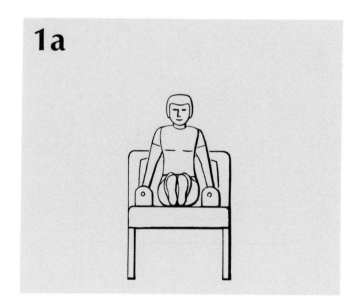

3

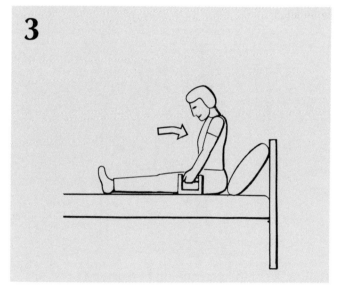

Repeat as many times as you need to, till you are in the correct position.

NOTE
1. *Make sure you keep your head bent forward all the time.*
2. *Illustrations shows moving up the bed only.*

MOVING UP OR DOWN BED
PARTLY ASSISTED
One helper required

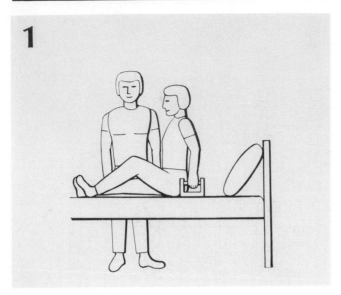

Person: Place block at left side just back from hip. Bend left leg up, keeping foot on bed.

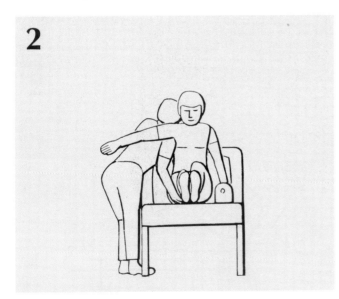

Helper: Put left hand behind person and press on bed. Put right hand beneath thigh of person.
Person: Put arm down the back of helper.

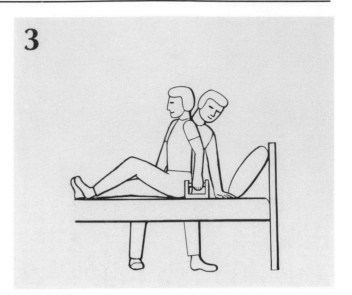

Helper: Make sure same foot as hand under thigh of person is pointing towards bed. Point other foot in line with direction of lift. Lean shoulder against person's chest below the armpit. Make sure head is between person and head of bed.

On command of '1–2–3–push'
Person: Dig heel in and push on block to lift buttocks through and back.
Helper: Press hand on bed and shoulder against person, lift and move up bed.

NOTE
1. *Helper assists on weak side, which in this example is the right side.*
2. *Helper must lean firmly into the person's chest throughout the lift.*
3. *This manoeuvre can also be used to move down the bed.*

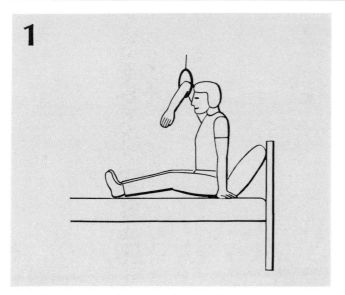

1

Hook arm through ring and press down on bed with other hand.

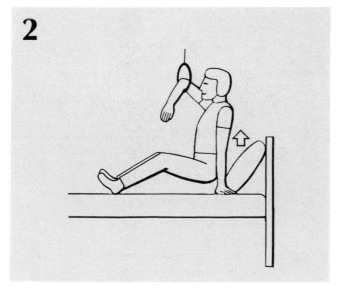

2

Pull on ring and push on hand, so that buttocks are raised clear of bed.

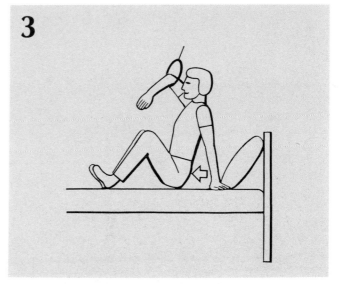

3

At the same time, move buttocks up or down bed.

NOTE
Alternatively, ring can be grasped in the hand.

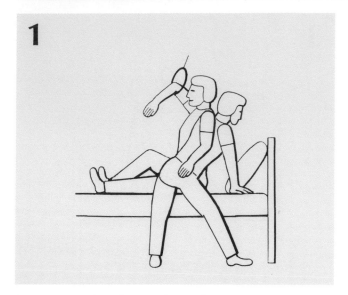

Person: Hook right arm through ring and place left arm down back of helper. Bend right leg.
Helper: Put right hand behind person and press on bed. Put left hand beneath thigh of person. Make sure left foot is pointing towards bed. Point right foot in line with direction of lift. Lean shoulder against person's chest below armpit. Make sure head is between person and head of bed.

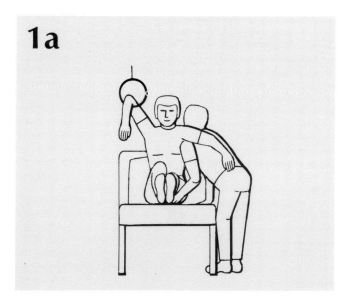

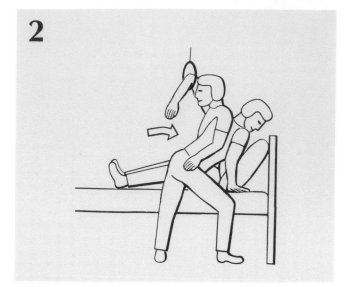

On command of '1–2–3–lift'
Person: Pull on ring and push on foot to raise buttocks.
Helper: Press hand on bed and shoulder against person and move person up or down bed.

NOTE
1. Helper must lean firmly into the person's chest throughout the lift.
2. Helper assists on weak side, which in this example is the left side.
3. Alternatively, ring can be grasped in the hand.

Linked arm support

1

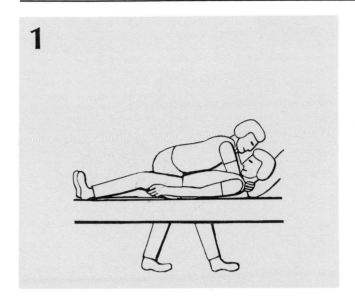

Helper: Crook right arm under right arm of person and put left hand at nape of neck.
Person: Clasp left hand under your left thigh.

2

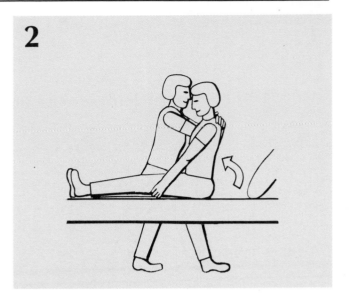

Helper: Make sure feet are pointing towards head of the bed with left foot forward.
On command '1–2–3–pull'
Helper: Lean backwards and push feet into floor, and help person to sit up.
Person: Pull on thigh.

NOTE
1. *Helper assists on weak side, which in this example is the right side.*
2. *This technique should be avoided if the person's shoulder is frail.*

1a

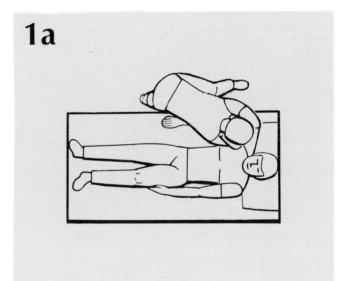

SITTING UP IN BED

MUCH ASSISTED
Two helpers required

1

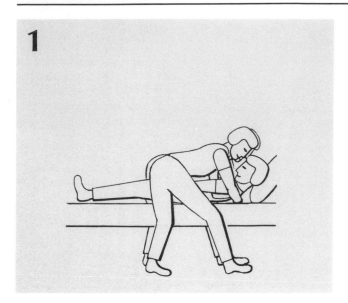

Helpers: Crook inner arm under arm of person, cradle shoulder and neck with other hand.

2

Helpers: Make sure your feet are pointing towards head of bed with outer foot forward. On command '1–2–3–pull' lean back and push feet into floor and help person to sit up.

1a

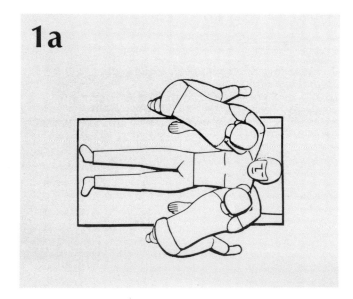

3

Helpers: Position pillow support behind person.

Shoulder lift

© Tony Pelosi and Margaret Gleeson 1988

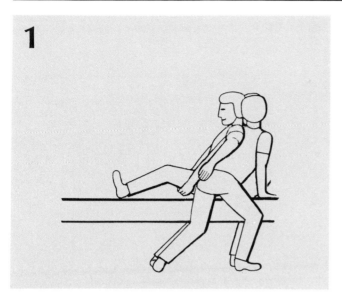

1

Helpers: Put one hand behind person press on bed. Put other hand beneath thighs of person and take a wrist grip with other helper.

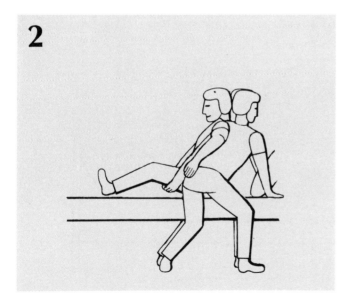

3

Helpers: Make sure head is between person and head of bed. On command '1–2–3–lift', press hand on bed and shoulder against person and move person a little way down the bed. Repeat until person has room to lie down.

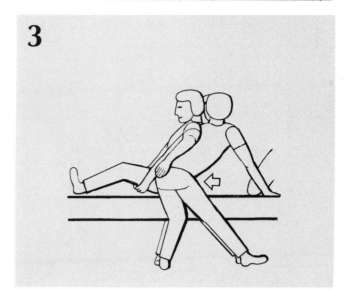

2

Helpers: Make sure same foot as hand under thigh of person is pointing towards bed. Point other foot towards head of bed. Lean shoulder against person's chest below armpit.
Person: Put arms down the backs of helpers, and keep head forward.

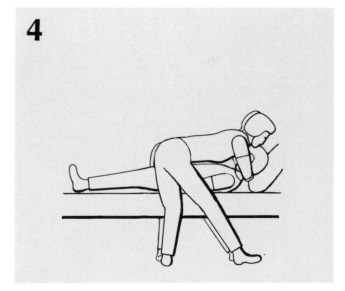

4

Helpers: Lie person back, gently supporting head and shoulders.

NOTE
Helpers must lean firmly into the person's chest throughout the lift.

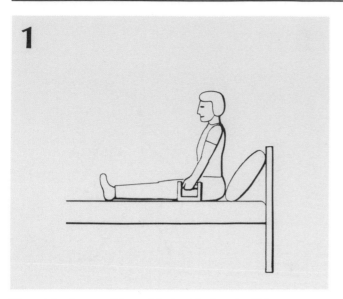

1

Place blocks on either side just in front of hips.

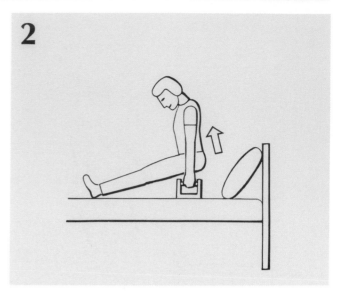

2

Bend forward. Push down with hands so that your buttocks lift off bed. Keep your head bent forward all the time.

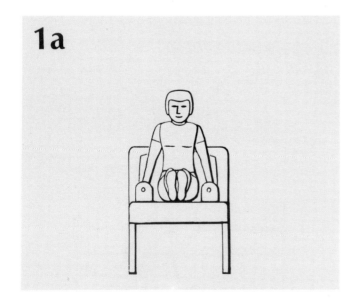

1a

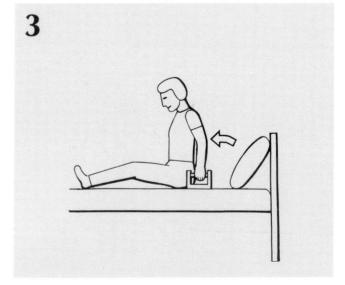

3

Swing buttocks forward and through. Repeat as many times as necessary for you to have enough room to lie back.

1

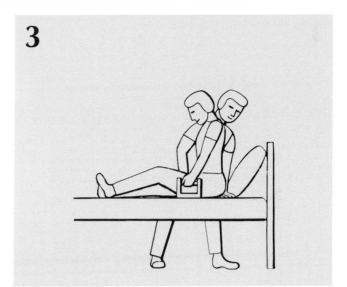

Person: Place block at left side, just in front of hip and slightly bend left leg up, keeping foot on bed.

2

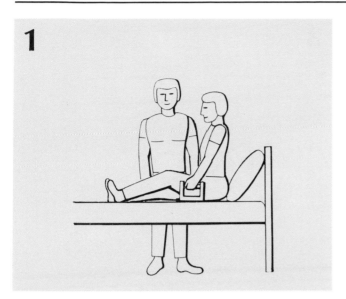

Helper: Put left hand behind person and press on bed. Put right hand beneath thigh of person.
Person: Put arm down the back of helper.

3

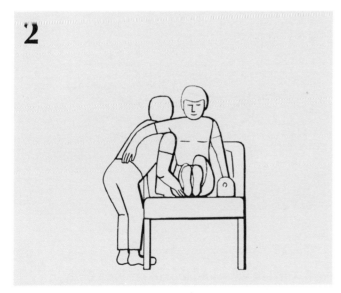

Helper: Make sure same foot as hand under thigh of person is pointing towards bed. Point other foot parallel to bed. Lean shoulder against person's chest below armpit. Make sure head is between person and head of bed.

4

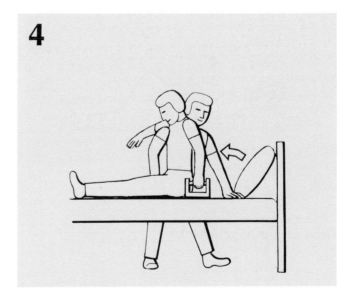

On command of '1–2–3–push'
Person: Dig heel in and push on block to lift buttocks through and forward.
Helper: Press hand on bed and shoulder against person, lift and move person down bed. Repeat as many times as necessary for person to have enough room to lie back.

NOTE
1. Helper assists on weak side which in this example is the right side.
2. Helper must lean firmly into the person's chest throughout the lift.

1

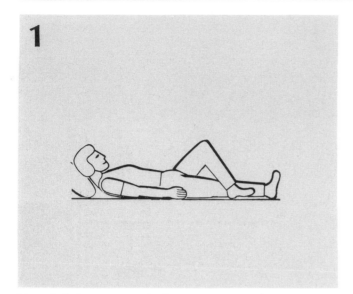

Place left foot over right foot.

2

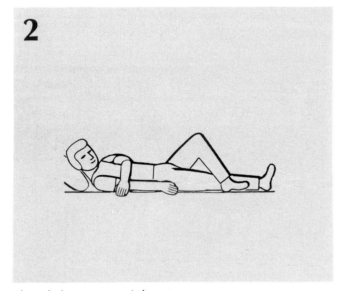

Place left arm over right arm.

3

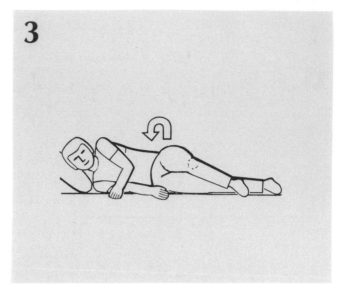

Pull on side of bed to roll onto right side.

4

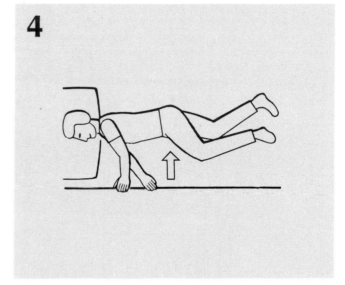

Push with left hand and foot to position body in middle of bed. Bend knees up to prevent rolling backwards.

NOTE
Reverse arm and leg positioning to roll to other side.

Limb cross-over

1

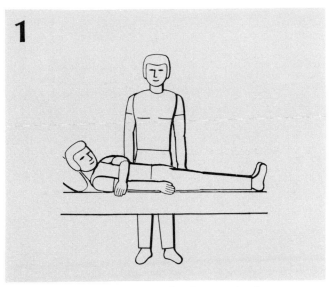

Person: Put left arm across body onto bed.

2

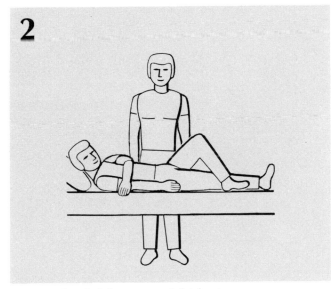

Person: Put left foot over right foot.

3

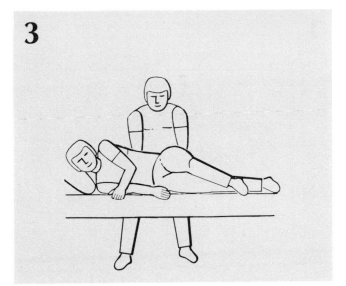

Helper: Put forearms under waist and below hips. Place feet wide apart with one foot forward and the other back.

4

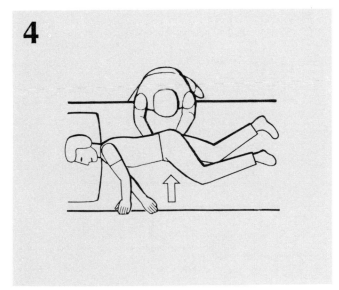

On command '1–2–3–push'
Helper: Brace your stomach and pull hips of person into middle of bed. Bend person's knees up to prevent rolling onto back.
Person: Push with left hand and foot to move into middle of bed.

MUCH ASSISTED
One helper required

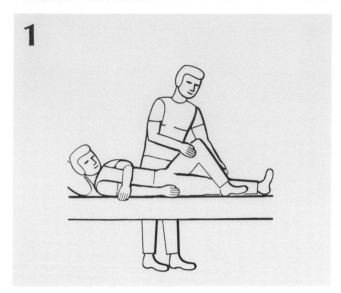

Helper: Assist person to place left arm over body onto bed and left foot over right foot.

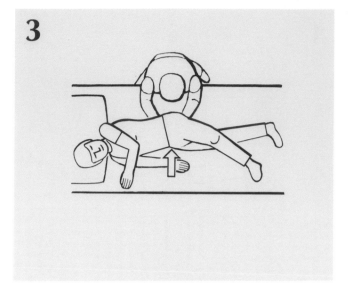

Helper: Brace your stomach and pull hips of person into middle of bed.

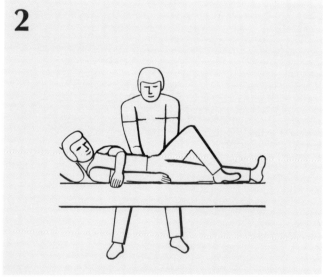

Helper: Put forearms under waist and below hips. Place feet wide apart with one foot forward and the other foot back.

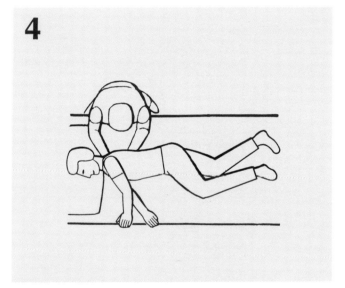

Helper: Put forearms under shoulders of person. Brace your stomach and move shoulders to middle of bed. Bend person's knees up to prevent rolling onto back.

NOTE
With a heavy person there should be a helper at the shoulders and one at the hips.

1

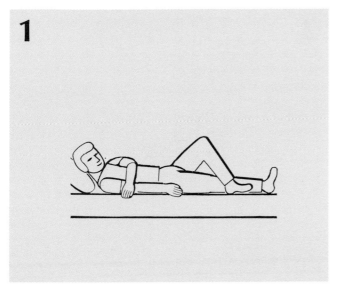

If on back, cross left leg over other leg, and left arm over body.

2

With left arm pull on edge of bed until you are on right side.

3

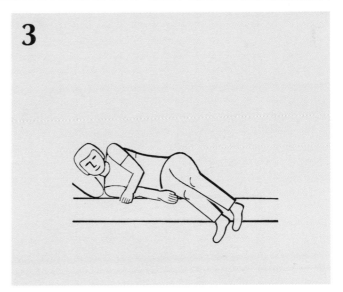

Bend knees up and put feet over edge of bed.

4

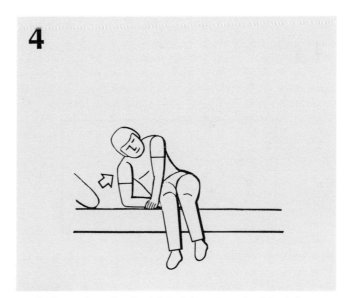

Push down into bed with left hand and with right elbow until sitting up.

NOTE
1. *Make sure you keep your head bent forward all the time until you are sitting up.*
2. *Movement should be led by the stronger side, which in this example is the left side.*

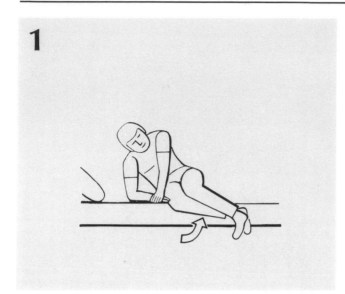

1

Lean down onto right elbow and use right leg to help left leg onto bed.

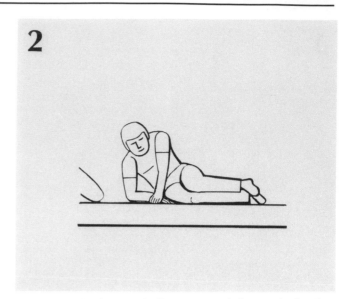

2

Lean on right foot and elbow to push buttocks back into middle of bed.

NOTE
1. *Make sure you keep your head bent forward.*
2. *Movement should be led by the stronger side, which in this example is the right side.*

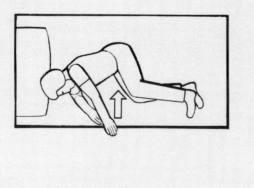

1a

LYING TO SITTING WITH LEGS OVER

PARTLY ASSISTED
One helper required

1

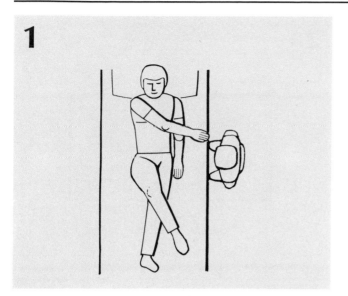

Person: Cross right leg over left leg and right arm over body.

2

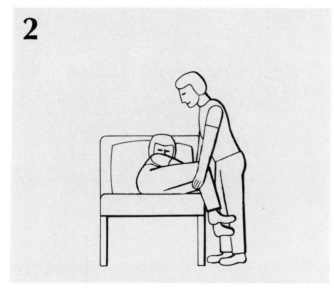

Helper: Bend person's knees so that feet are over edge of bed and person is on left side.

3

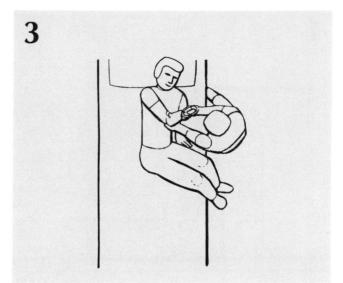

Helper: Stand on left side of person at an angle of 45°. Right foot forward. Grasp person's elbow in your left hand and right hand in thumb-through grip.

4

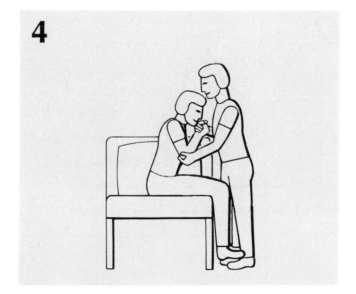

Helper: Squat slightly.
On command of '1–2–3–pull'
Helper: Straighten your knees and help person into sitting position.
Person: Bend head forward and pull on helper's hand.

NOTE
1. *Person should keep head bent forward throughout this manoeuvre.*
2. *Assistance is given on the stronger side, which in this example is the right side.*

SITTING WITH LEGS OVER, TO LYING

PARTLY ASSISTED
One helper required

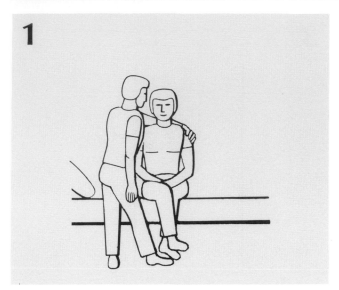

Helper: Stand on person's right side, with left foot pointing towards bed and right foot towards person's feet. Cradle neck and shoulder in left arm.
Person: Cross right foot over left foot.

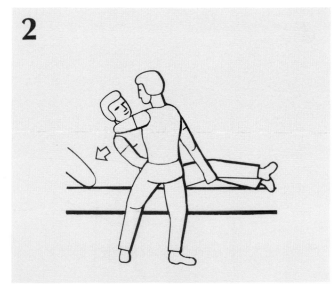

On command '1–2–3–ready'
Person: Lie down onto right side.
Helper: Bend your knees and put right arm under legs of person. Assist legs onto bed as person lies down onto right side.

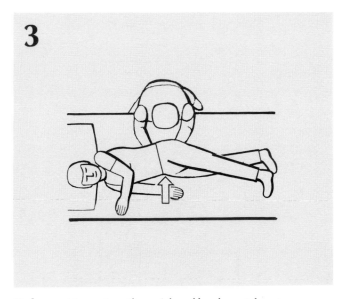

Helper: Move to other side of bed, put forearms under waist and thighs of person.
On command '1–2–3–push'
Person: Push down on bed with left hand and foot.
Helper: Brace your stomach and pull person's hips towards middle of bed.

NOTE
1. *Assistance is given on the weaker side, which in this example is the right side.*
2. *In order to gain the leverage of this transfer it is essential that assistance from the helper is given as soon as the person begins to lie down.*

LYING TO SITTING WITH LEGS OVER
MUCH ASSISTED
Two helpers required

1

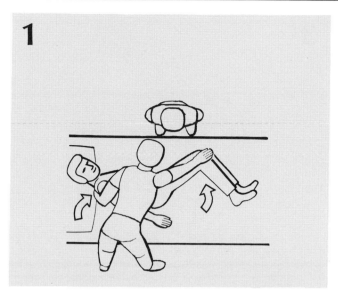

Helper 1: Bend person's knees up and roll knees towards other helper. At the same time, assist by pushing behind right shoulder-blade so that trunk rolls too.

2

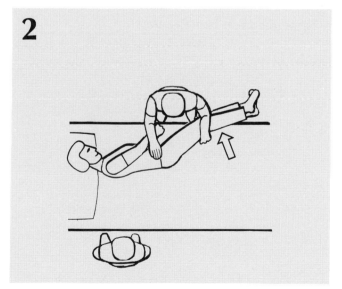

Helper 2: Put person's feet over edge of bed whilst keeping person rolled onto left side.

3

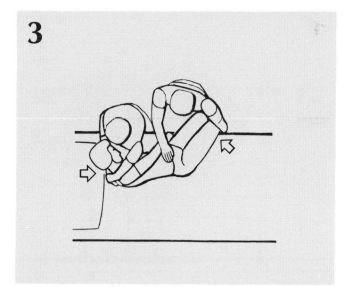

Helpers: Face bed, one each side of person, same side of bed.
Helper 1: Cradle person's neck and shoulder in right arm and support person's right shoulder blade with left hand.
Helper 2: Block person's knees and left hip.

4

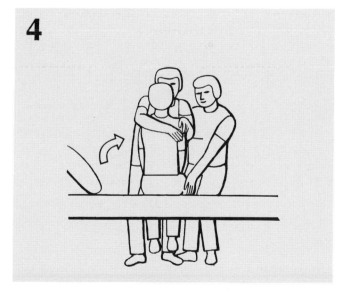

On command '1–2–3–lift'
Helper 2: Lever person's legs down and be ready to prevent person falling over.
Helper 1: Squat down a little and stand up to lift person into sitting.

NOTE
Keep person's head bent forward.

35

SITTING WITH LEGS OVER, TO LYING

MUCH ASSISTED
Two helpers required

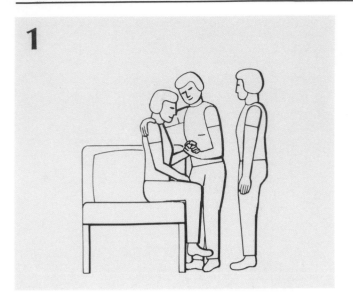

Helper 1: Face person sitting on bed. Hold person's left hand in a thumb-through grip and cradle person's neck and shoulders in your right arm.
Helper 2: Help person balance if necessary.

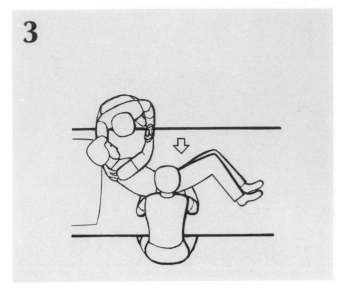

Helper 2: Move round to other side of bed. Put forearms under person's waist and thighs. Brace your stomach and pull hips to move person towards middle of bed.

NOTE
Keep person's head bent forward.

On command '1–2–3–ready'
Helper 1: Slowly lower person onto bed. Keep person's head bent forward.
Helper 2: Lift legs up onto bed.

Bed/chair transfers

5

© Tony Pelosi and Margaret Gleeson 1988

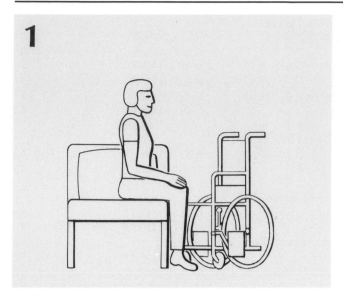

1

Park chair at 45° angle to bed. Brakes on, near side arm-rest removed and footplates swung away.

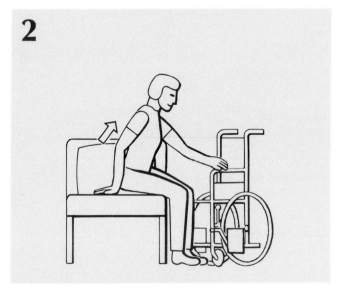

2

Put left hand on arm rest and right hand on bed. Keep left foot slightly forward.

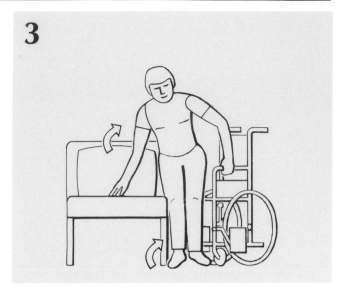

3

Lean forward and push up to lift buttocks. Pivot feet around, until facing away from chair.

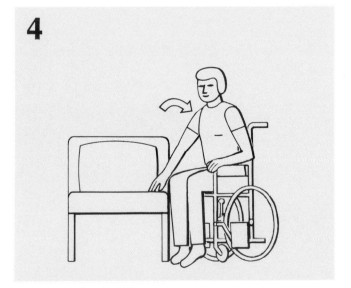

4

Make sure backs of legs are against chair before sitting down.

NOTE
1. *Movement should be in the direction of the stronger side, which is the left side in this example.*
2. *A rotating board may be useful (see Ch.3).*

© Tony Pelosi and Margaret Gleeson 1988

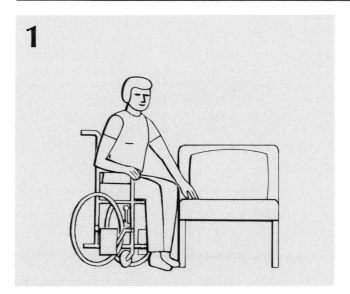

1

Park chair at 45° angle to bed. Brakes on, near side-arm rest removed and footplates swung away. Put left hand on bed and right hand on arm-rest. Keep left foot slightly forward.

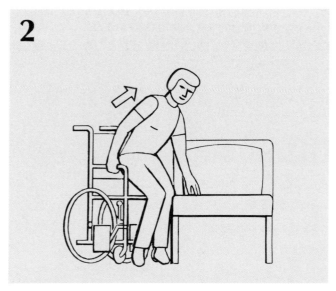

2

Lean forward and push up to lift buttocks.

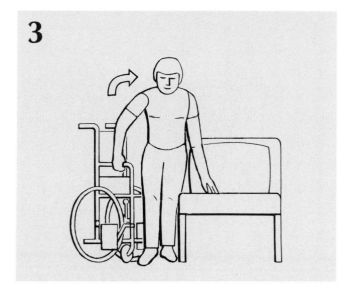

3

Pivot feet around until facing away from bed.

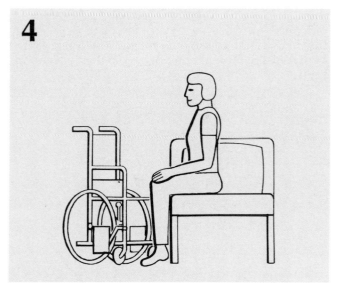

4

Make sure backs of legs are against bed before sitting down.

NOTE
1. *Movement should be in the direction of the stronger side, which is the left side in this example.*
2. *A rotating board may be useful (see Ch.3).*

BED TO CHAIR

PARTLY ASSISTED
One helper required

1

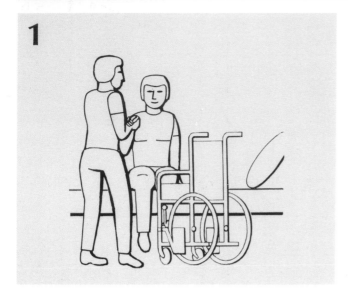

Park chair at 45° angle to bed. Brakes on, near side arm-rest removed and footplates swung away.
Helper: Stand on person's right side. Take thumb-through grip with person's right hand and hold person's right elbow with your left hand. Point right foot in direction of movement, and left foot at 45° to bed. Assist person to edge of bed so that feet are on floor.

2

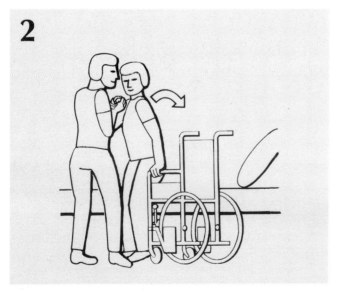

Person: Put left hand on far side arm-rest. Keep left foot slightly forward.
On command '1–2–3–stand'
Person: Pull on hand grip to stand up and pivot feet around until facing away from chair.
Helper: Allow person to take weight on hand to assist person to stand and pivot.

3

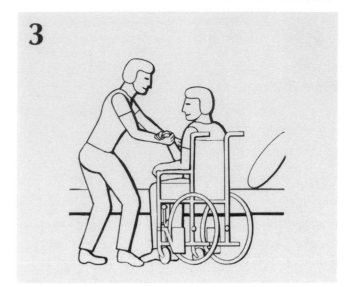

Make sure back of person's legs are against chair before sitting down.
Helper: Lunge toward chair as person sits down.

NOTE
1. *Movement should be in the direction of the stronger side, which is the left side in this example.*
2. *A rotating board may be useful (see Ch.3).*

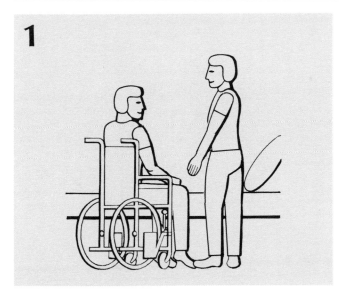

Park chair at 45° angle to bed. Brakes on, near side arm-rest removed and footplates swung away.
Helper: Stand with right thigh alongside bed and right foot pointing under bed. Point left foot to person.

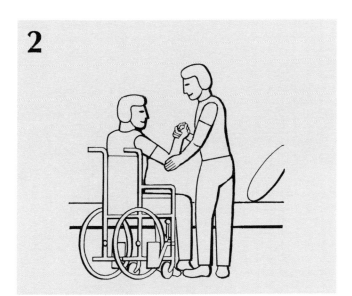

Helper: Take a thumb-through grip with person's right hand and hold person's right elbow with your left hand. Assist person to front of chair.
Person: Put left hand onto bed and keep left foot slightly forward.

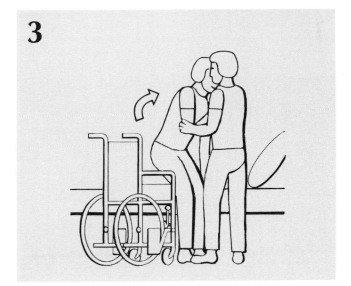

On command '1–2–3–stand'
Person: Pull on gripped hand to stand up and pivot feet around, until facing away from bed.
Helper: Allow person to take weight on hand to assist person to stand and pivot.

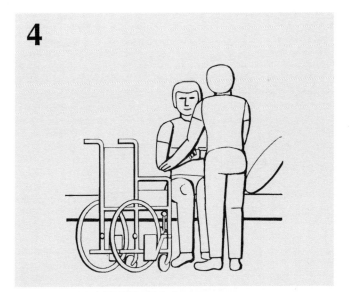

Make sure backs of person's legs are against bed before sitting down.
Helper: Lunge towards bed as person sits down.

NOTE
1. *Movement should be in direction of stronger side, which is the left side in this example.*
2. *A rotating board may be useful (see Ch.3).*

MUCH ASSISTED
One helper required

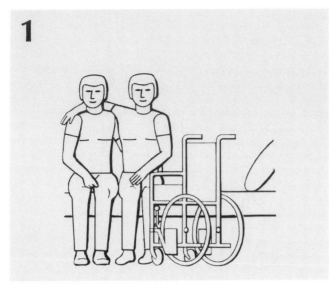

1

Park chair at 45° angle to bed. Brakes on, near side arm-rest removed and footplates swung away.
Helper: Sit on bed with right arm of person over your shoulder. Put your left arm around person's back and grasp waistband.

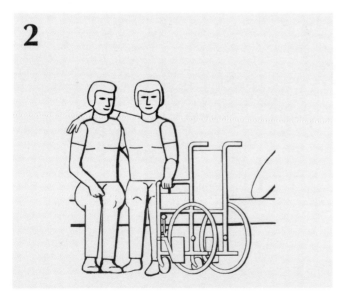

2

Person: Put the left hand on the far side arm rest. Keep the left foot slightly forward.

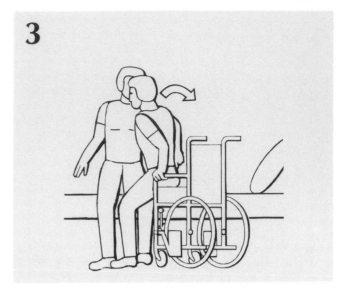

3

On command '1–2–3–stand', stand up together.
Person: Pivot feet around, until facing away from chair.
Helper: Shuffle feet around while person pivots.

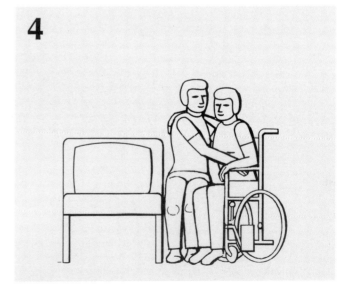

4

Helper: Make sure backs of person's legs are against chair before squatting down to assist person to sit in chair.

NOTE
1. *Movement should be in the direction of the stronger side, which is the left side in this example.*
2. *A rotating board may be useful (see Ch.3).*
3. *This manoeuvre should only be used when helper and person are similar in size.*

© Tony Pelosi and Margaret Gleeson 1988

1

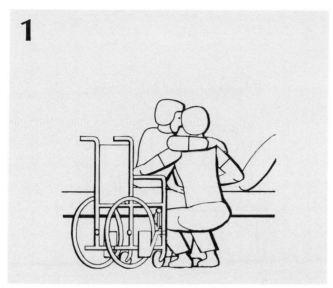

Park chair at 45° angle to bed. Brakes on, near side arm-rest removed and footplates swung away. Leave room for helper.
Helper: Crouch beside person's right side and put person's right arm over your shoulder. Put your left arm around person's back and grasp waistband.
Person: Put left hand on bed. Keep left foot slightly forward.

2

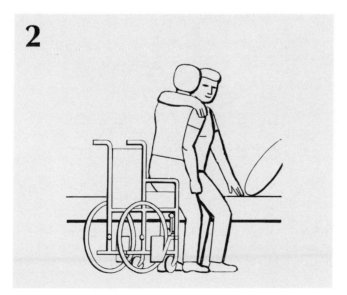

On command '1–2–3–stand', Stand up together.
Person: Pivot feet around, until facing away from bed.
Helper: Shuffle feet around while person pivots.

3

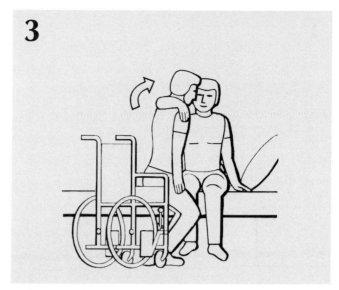

Helper: Make sure backs of person's legs are against bed before squatting down to assist person to sit on bed.

NOTE
1. *Movement should be in the direction of the stronger side, which is the left in this example.*
2. *A rotating board may be useful (see Ch.3).*
3. *This manoeuvre should only be used when helper and person are similar in size.*

MUCH ASSISTED
One helper required

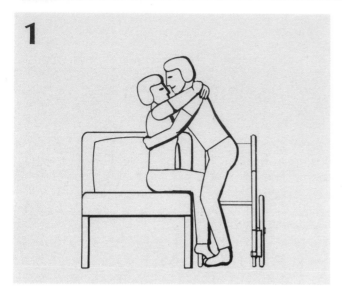

Park chair alongside bed. Brakes on, near side arm-rest removed and footplates swung away.
Helper: Help person forward towards edge of bed. Take person in a shoulder-blade grip, and position feet and knees so that person's feet and knees are blocked from slipping forward or bending.
Person: Put arms around shoulders of helper.

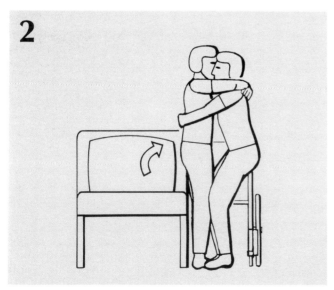

Helper: Squat down slightly.
On command '1–2–3–stand'
Helper: Make sure of balance, and stand up to assist person to stand.
Person: Keep head bent forward and grip on shoulder of helper to stand up.

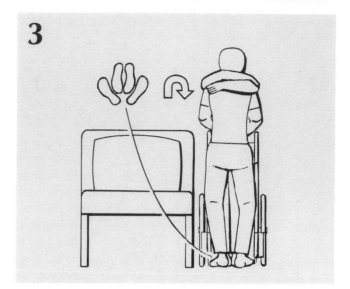

When balanced, together pivot slowly around, making sure person's knees are prevented from bending.

Helper: Make sure backs of person's legs are against chair before sitting. Put one hand on front of person's hip and push forward to help person sit down.

NOTE
A rotating board may be useful (see Ch.3).

© Tony Pelosi and Margaret Gleeson 1988

1

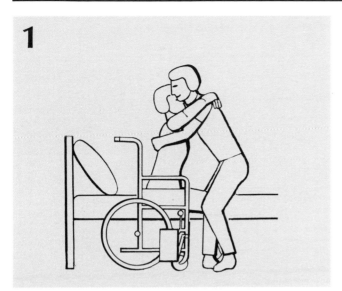

Park chair alongside bed. Brakes on, near side arm-rest removed and footplates swung away.
Helper: Help person forward towards edge of chair. Take person in a shoulder blade grip and position feet and knees so that person's feet and knees are blocked from slipping forward or bending.
Person: Put arms around shoulders of helper.

2

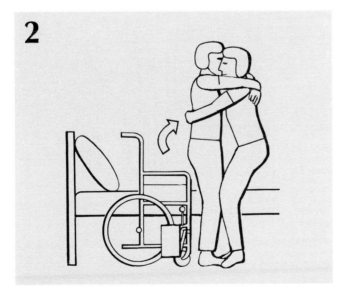

Helper: Squat down slightly.
On command '1–2–3–stand'
Helper: Make sure of balance, and stand up to assist person to stand.
Person: Keep head bent forward and grip shoulders of helper to stand up.

3

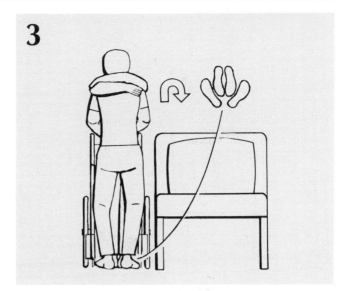

When balanced, together pivot around, making sure person's knees are prevented from bending.

4

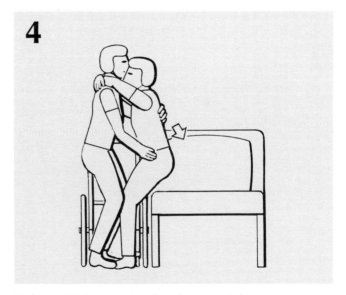

Helper: Make sure backs of person's legs are against bed before sitting. Put one hand on front of person's hip and push forward to help person sit down on bed.

NOTE
A rotating board may be useful (see Ch.3).

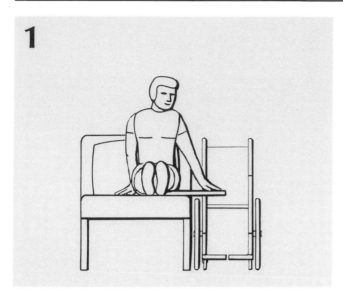

1

Park chair parallel to and against bed. Brakes on and near side arm-rest removed. Place slide board under left buttock and on chair. Put left hand on end of slide board and right hand beside right hip.

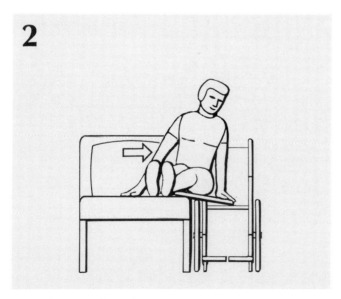

2

Push down on board and bed, and slide along board onto chair.

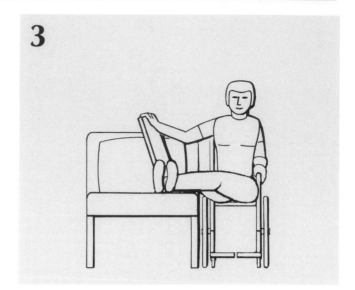

3

Leave feet on bed. Remove slide board.

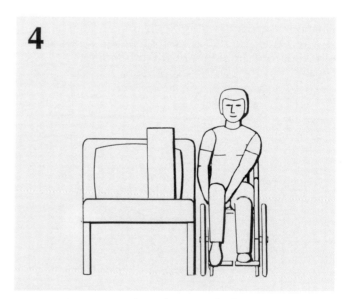

4

Put feet down onto footplates and adjust sitting position.

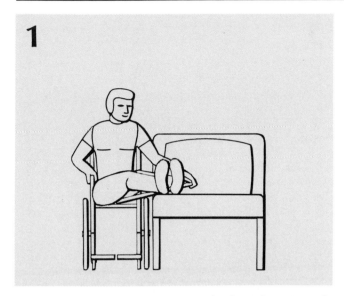

1

Park chair parallel to and against bed. Brakes on and near side arm-rest removed. Put feet up onto bed. Place slide board under left buttock and on bed.

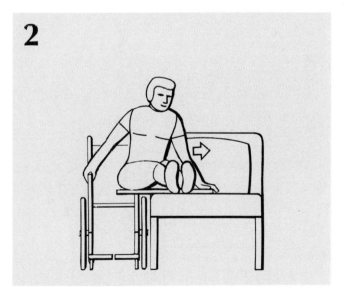

3

Remove slide board.

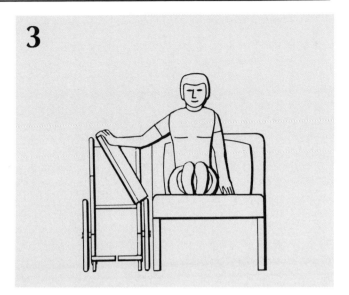

2

Put right hand on arm-rest and left hand on end of slide board. Push down on hands, and slide along board onto bed.

PARTLY ASSISTED
One helper required

© Tony Pelosi and Margaret Gleeson 1988

1

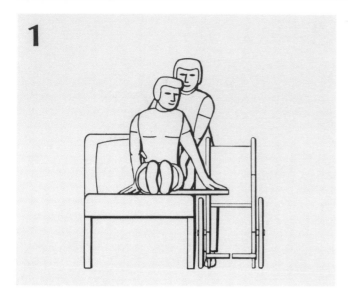

Park chair parallel to and against bed. Brakes on and near side arm-rest removed.
Person: Place slide board under left buttock and on chair. Put right hand on bed next to right hip. Left hand on end of slide board.
Helper: Stand behind chair with right knee on bed and left foot pointing to the chair. Grasp waistband of person.

1a

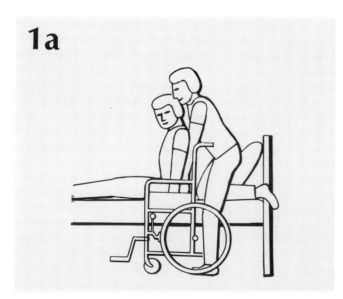

2

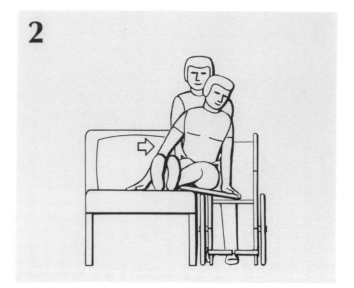

On command '1–2–3–push'
Person: Push down on board and bed, and slide along board onto chair.
Helper: Using waistband assist person to slide along board onto chair.

3

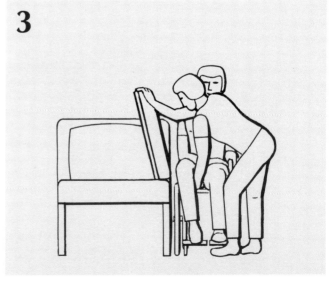

Helper: Remove board, lift legs from bed and place feet on footplates.

NOTE
A seat belt can be used if there is no waistband (see Ch.3).

1

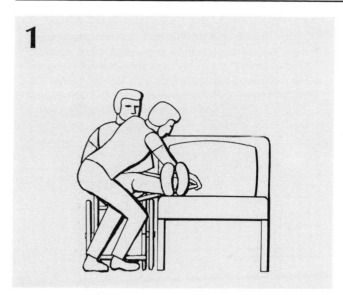

Park chair parallel to and against bed. Brakes on and near side arm-rest removed.
Helper: Put person's feet up onto bed. Place slide board under left buttock and on bed.

2

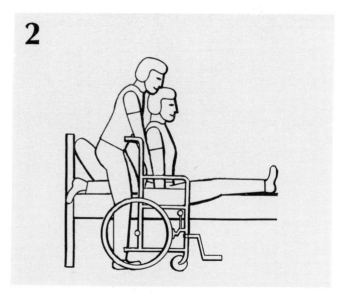

Helper: Stand behind person with right foot pointing to chair and left knee on bed. Grasp person's waistband.

3

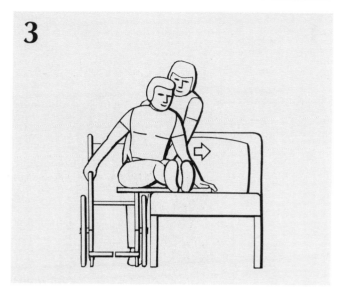

Person: Put right hand on arm rest and left hand on end of slide board.
On command '1–2–3–push'
Helper: Use waistband to assist person to slide along board onto bed.
Person: Push down on board and arm rest and slide along board.

4

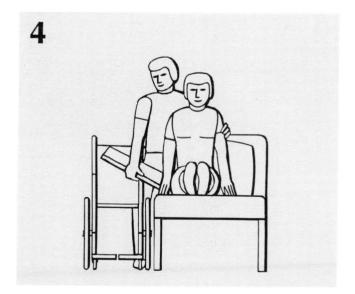

Helper: Remove board.

NOTE
A seat belt can be used if there is no waistband (see Ch.3).

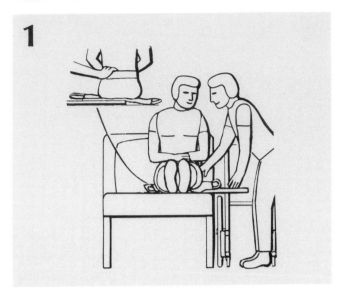

1

Park chair parallel to and against bed. Brakes on, near side arm-rest removed and footplates swung away.
Helper: Make sure slide board mat is properly in place, and secure belt around person's waist. Place slide board well under mat and other end on wheelchair.

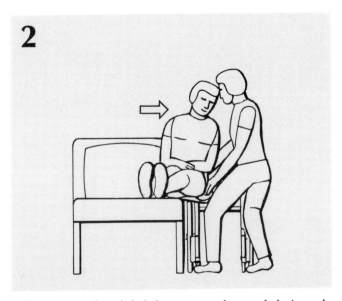

2

Helper: Stand with left foot across front of chair and right foot at far side of chair, both pointing to the bed. Hold mat handle with left hand, and belt with right hand. Bend knees. Pull on the mat handle and belt, and slowly slide person along board and into chair.

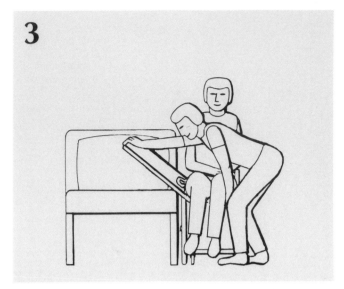

3

Helper: Remove board. Put person's feet down onto footplates.

NOTE
If this transfer cannot be performed safely, use another helper to assist with balance, or use a hoist.

1

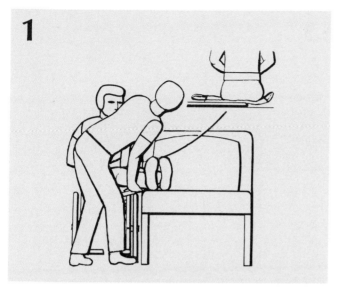

Park chair parallel to and against the bed. Brakes on and near side arm-rest removed.
Helper: Put person's feet onto bed. Place one end of slide board under mat, and other end on bed. Secure belt around person's waist.

2

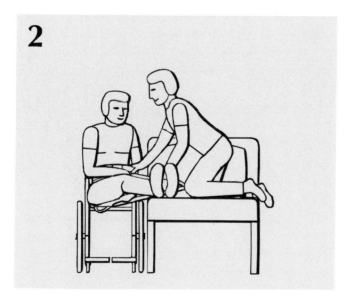

Helper: Move around to other side of bed. Kneel on bed with left knee forward. Grasp belt with right hand and mat with left hand.

3

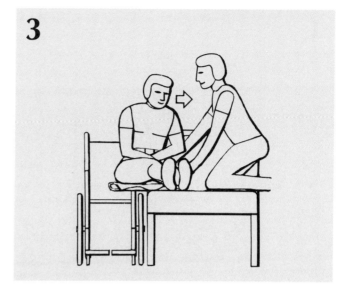

Helper: Pull on belt and mat handle at the same time and slowly slide person along board and onto bed

NOTE
If this transfer cannot be performed safely, use another helper to assist with balance, or use a hoist.

PARTLY ASSISTED
One helper required

1

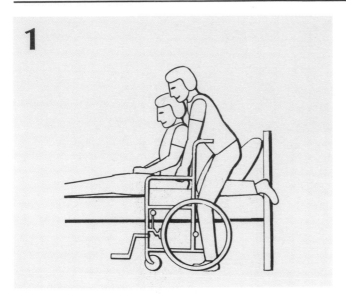

Park chair parallel to and against bed. Brakes on and near side arm-rest removed.
Helper: Stand behind chair with right knee on bed and left foot pointing towards chair. Grasp waistband of person.

3

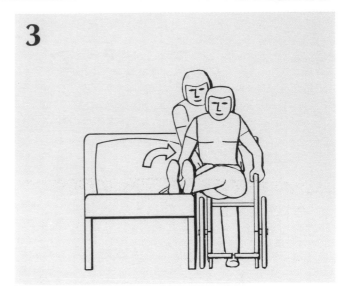

On command '1–2–3–push'
Person: Push down on hands to lift buttocks up and over onto chair.
Helper: Use waistband to assist person to hitch buttocks onto chair. Leave feet on bed.

2

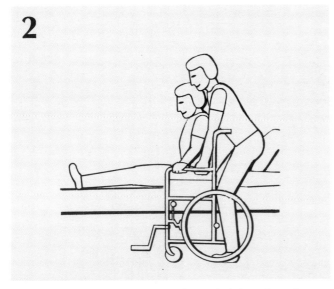

Person: Move to edge of bed. Put left hand on far side arm-rest and right hand on bed beside hip.

4

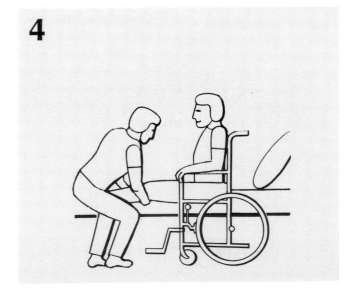

Helper: Move around to front and assist in putting person's feet on footplates.

NOTE
1. Movement should be in the direction of the stronger side, which is the left side in this example.
2. A seat belt can be used if there is no waistband (see Ch.3).

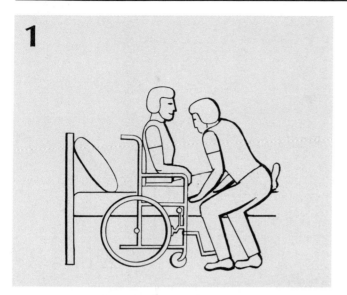

1

Park chair parallel to and against bed. Brakes on and near side arm-rest removed.
Helper: Put person's feet on bed.

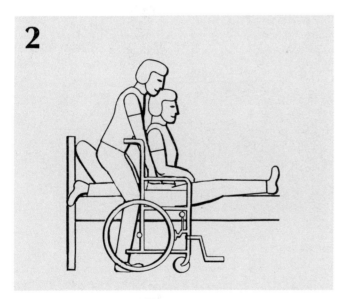

2

Helper: Move around behind chair. Put left knee on bed and point right foot under the chair. Grasp person's waistband.

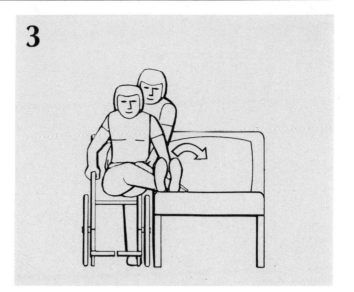

3

Person: Put left hand on bed and right hand on arm rest.
On command '1–2–3–push'
Person: Push down on hands to raise buttocks up and over onto bed.
Helper: Use waistband to assist person to hitch buttocks onto bed.

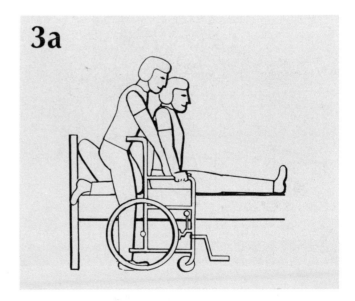

3a

NOTE
1. Movement should be in the direction of the stronger side, which is the left side in this example.
2. A seat belt can be used if there is no waistband (see Ch.3).

1

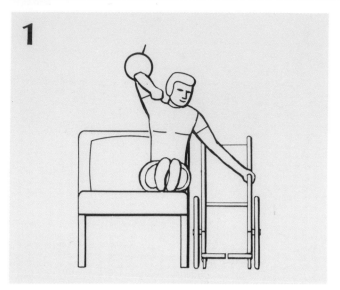

Park chair parallel to and against bed. Brakes on and near side arm-rest removed. Hook right arm through ring. Put left hand on arm-rest of chair.

3

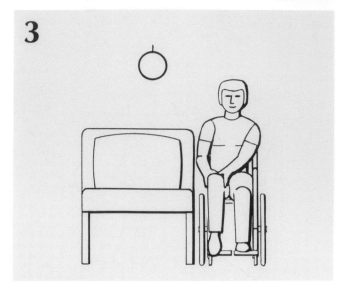

Lift legs from bed and put feet down on footplates.

NOTE
Alternatively, ring can be grasped with the hand.

2

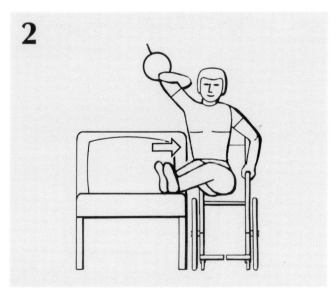

Push on left hand and pull on arm to lift buttocks up. Swing onto chair leaving feet in bed.

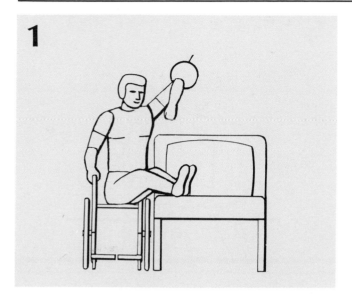

1

Park chair parallel to and against bed. Brakes on and near side arm-rest removed. Put feet up onto bed and hook left arm through ring. Put right hand on arm rest.

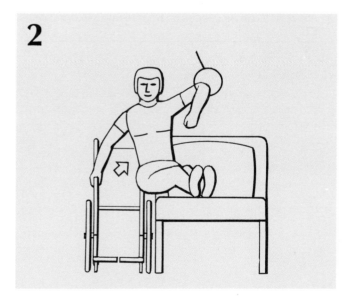

2

Push up on right hand, pull on left arm to raise buttocks up and over onto bed.

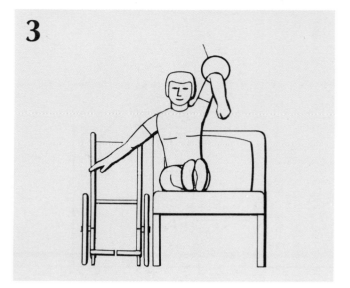

3

Lower onto bed.

NOTE
1. Alternatively, ring can be grasped with the hand.
2. Movement should be in the direction of stronger side, which is the left side in this example.

PARTLY ASSISTED
One helper required

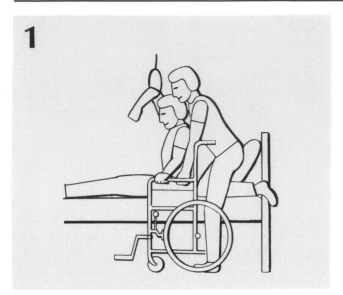

Park chair parallel to and against bed. Brakes on and near side arm-rest removed.
Person: Hook right arm through ring and put left hand on arm-rest.
Helper: Stand behind chair with right knee on bed and left foot pointing towards the chair. Grasp person's waistband.

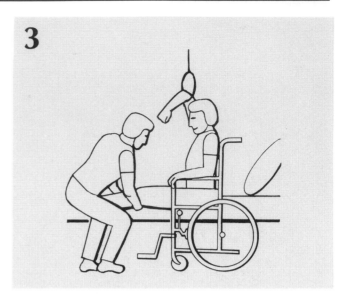

On command '1–2–3–lift'
Person: Push down on left hand and pull on right arm to raise buttocks.
Helper: Use waistband to assist person to raise buttocks and to swing over onto the chair. Leave feet on bed.

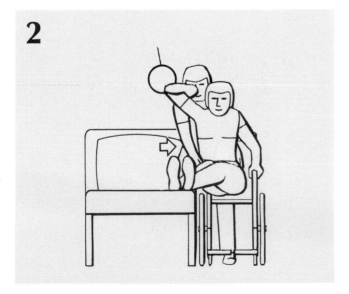

Helper: Move around to the front and put person's feet on footplates.

NOTE
1. Alternatively, ring can be grasped with the hand.
2. A seat belt can be used instead of the waistband (see Ch.3).

CHAIR TO BED
PARTLY ASSISTED
One helper required

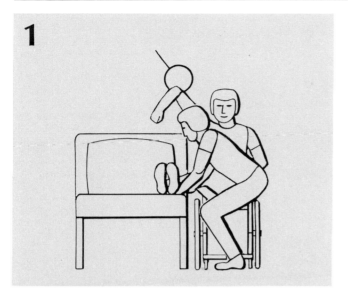

1

Park chair parallel to and against bed. Brakes on and near side arm-rest removed.
Person: Hook right arm through ring and put left hand on arm rest.
Helper: Put person's feet onto bed.

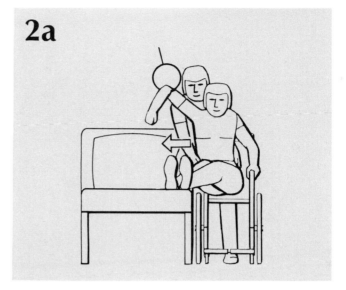

2a

NOTE
1. Alternatively, ring can be grasped with the hand.
2. A seat belt can be used instead of the waistband (see Ch.3).

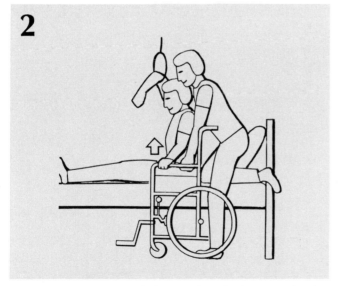

2

Helper: Stand behind chair with right knee on bed and left foot pointing towards chair. Grasp person's waistband.
On command '1–2–3–lift'
Person: Push on left hand and pull on right arm to raise buttocks.
Helper: Use waistband to assist person to lift buttocks and swing person over onto bed.

BED TO CHAIR
MUCH ASSISTED
Two helpers required

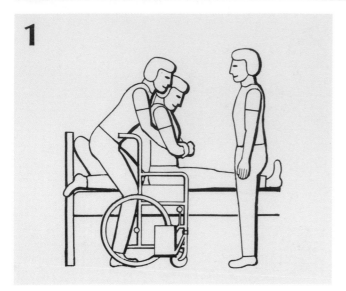

1

Park chair parallel to and against bed. Brakes on, near side arm-rest removed and footplates swung away.
Helper 1: Stand behind chair on bed side of wheelchair handles. Put bed side knee on bed, point other foot in direction of chair and bend knee slightly. Take person in a through-arm, wrist crossed-over grip.

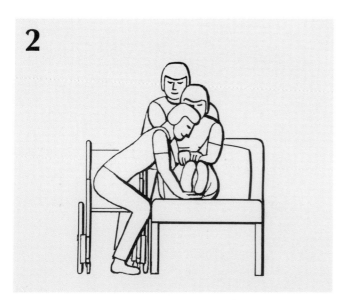

2

Helper 2: Stand facing bed with knees bent. Slide one hand under person's thighs, and the other under heels.

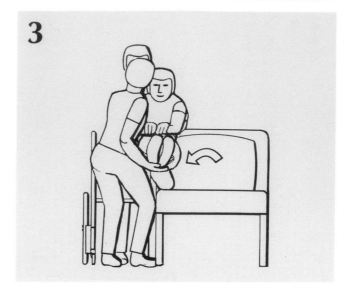

3

On command '1–2–3–lift'
Helper 1: Lift person up and onto chair, by rocking your weight from bed to supporting leg.
Helper 2: Straighten knees and lift person over to chair. Squat down to lower person into the chair. If necessary, take a couple of steps backwards between bed and chair.

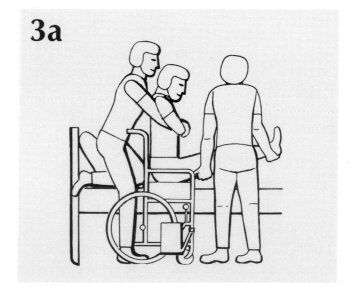

3a

NOTE
The taller helper should be behind the chair.

58

1

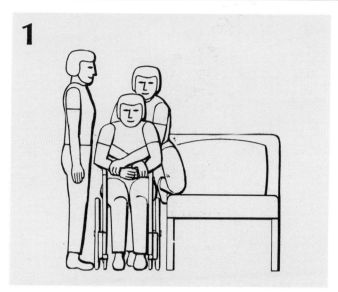

Park chair parallel to and against bed. Brakes on, near side arm-rest removed and footplates swung away.
Helper 1: Stand behind chair on bed side of wheelchair handles. Put bed side knee on bed, point other foot in direction of chair and bend knee slightly. Take person in a through-arm, wrist crossed-over grip.

2

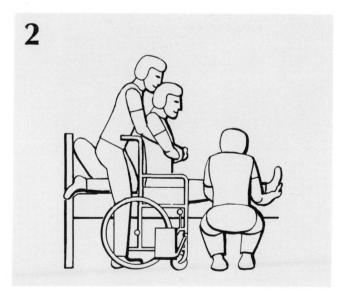

Helper 2: Squat down beside person's legs facing bed. Slide one hand under person's thighs and other hand under heels.

3

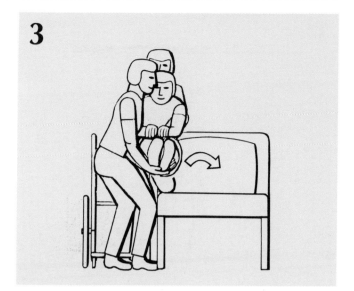

On command '1–2–3–lift'
Helper 1: Straighten supporting leg and rock weight over onto bed side knee as you lift person up and over onto bed.
Helper 2: Straighten your knees and lift person up and over onto bed. If necessary, take a couple of steps forward between chair and bed.

3a

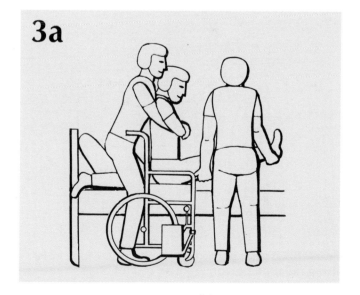

NOTE
The taller helper should be behind the chair.

59

1

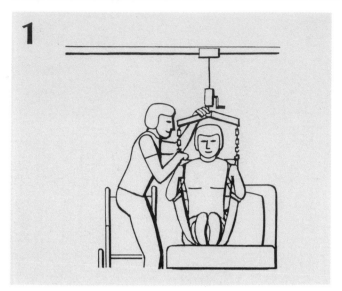

Park chair parallel to and against bed, underneath rail in ceiling. Brakes on, near side arm-rest removed and footplates swung away. Position sling(s) under person and attach sling(s) to hooks of hoist.

3

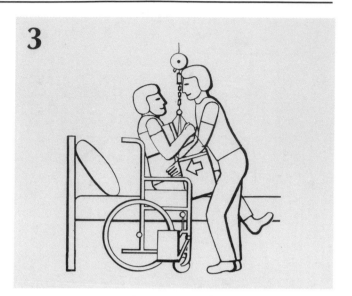

Lower person into chair and just before making contact with chair, push on person's hip towards back of chair to obtain the best sitting position. Remove sling(s).

2

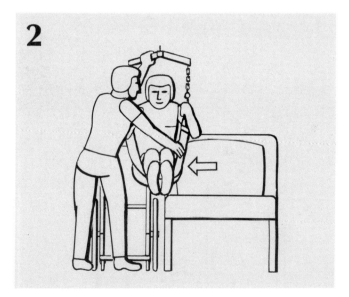

Crank hoist until person is clear of bed. Move hoist along rail until person is above seat of chair.

© Tony Pelosi and Margaret Gleeson 1988

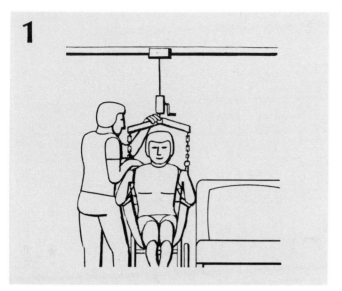

Park chair parallel to and against bed, underneath rail in ceiling. Brakes on, near side arm-rest removed and footplates swung away. Position sling(s) under person and attach sling(s) to hooks of hoist.

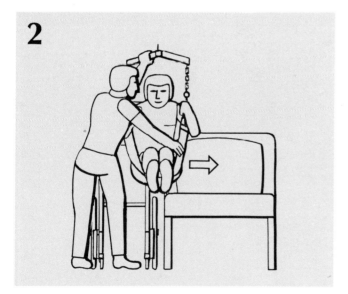

Crank up hoist until person is clear of chair and bed. Slide hoist across rail until person is over middle of bed.

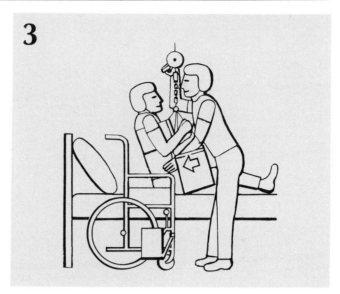

Lower person down gently onto bed. Remove sling(s).

BED TO CHAIR

MUCH ASSISTED
One helper required

1

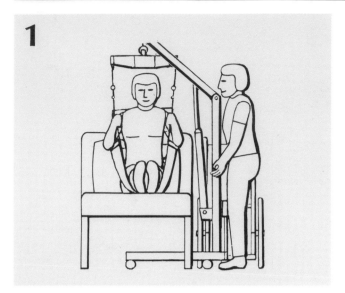

Park chair alongside bed. Brakes on, near side arm-rest removed and footplates swung away. Position sling(s) under person and attach sling(s) to hooks of mobile hoist.

2

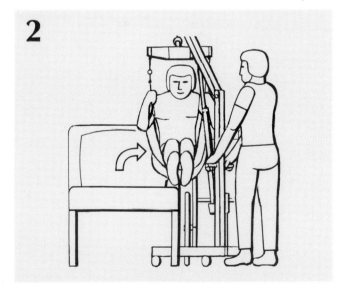

Crank hoist until person is clear of bed. Move mobile hoist so that person is above seat of chair. Put brakes on.

3

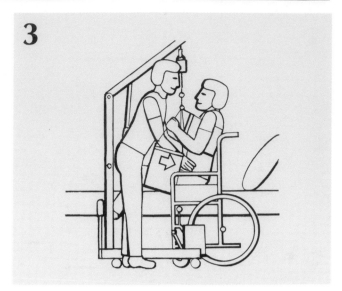

Lower person into chair and just before making contact with the seat push on person's hip towards back of chair to obtain best sitting position. Remove sling(s).

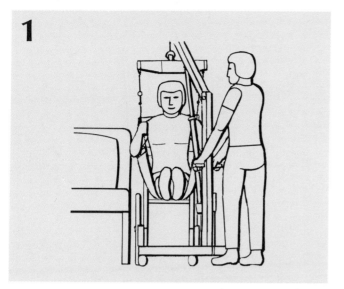

1

Park chair alongside bed. Brakes on, near side arm-rest removed and footplates swung away. Position sling(s) under person and attach sling(s) to hooks on hoist.

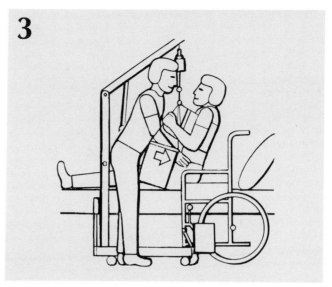

3

Gently lower person down onto bed. Remove sling(s).

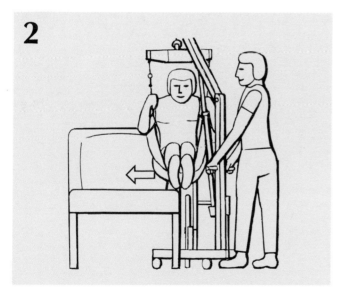

2

Crank hoist until person is clear of chair and bed. Move mobile hoist so that person is over the middle of the bed. Put brakes on.

Chair/toilet transfers

6

Depending on their various abilities, people can arrange their clothing for toiletting with varying degrees of independence. We have therefore not attempted to describe optimum methods of so doing. However, it is a general safety rule to avoid actually transferring with clothing undone.

1

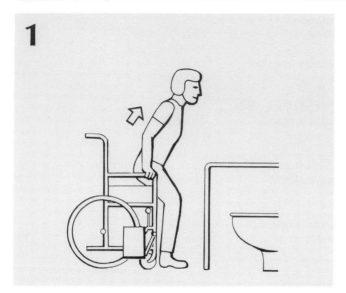

Park chair facing the toilet, brakes on and footplates swung away. Put both hands on arms of chair and push up into standing.

2

Put left hand onto diagonally opposite rail. Walk feet around to face in opposite direction.

3

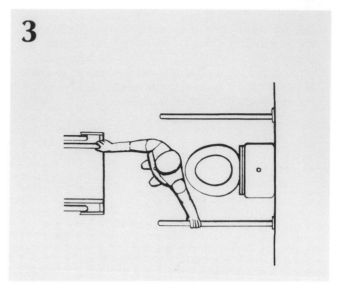

Move right hand first to other arm-rest and then to other rail.

4

Arrange clothing. Make sure back of legs are against toilet bowl, then sit down.

NOTE
1. *Because toilet areas are usually small, this transfer is shown, but where space permits, park the chair at a 45° angle to the toilet.*
2. *An overpedestal stool with hand supports can be used as an alternative to rails.*
3. *Movement should be in the direction of the stronger side, which in this example is the left.*
4. *A rotating board may be useful (see Ch. 3).*

© Tony Pelosi and Margaret Gleeson 1988

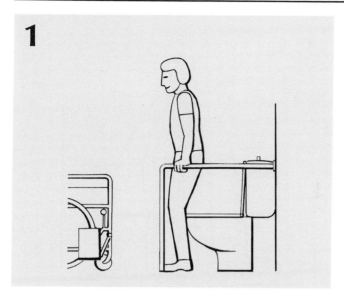

Park chair facing toilet, brakes on and footplates swung away. Put hands on rails and pull up into standing. Arrange clothing.

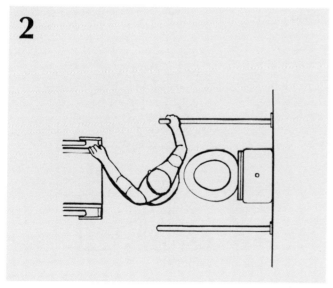

Put left hand onto diagonally opposite arm-rest. Walk feet around to face in opposite direction.

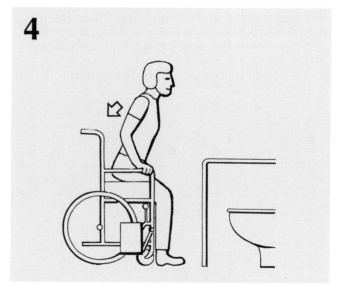

Move right hand first to other rail and then to arm-rest as you pivot around.

Make sure back of legs are against the chair before sitting.

NOTE
1. Because toilet areas are usually small, this transfer is shown, but where space permits, park chair at a 45° angle to the toilet.
2. An overpedestal stool with hand supports can be used as an alternative to rails.
3. Movement should be in the direction of the stronger side which is the left in this example.
4. A rotating board may be useful (see Ch. 3).

CHAIR TO TOILET

PARTLY ASSISTED
One helper required

© Tony Pelosi and Margaret Gleeson 1988

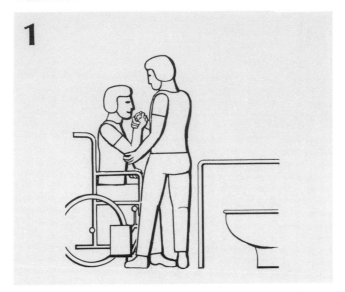

Park chair facing the toilet, brakes on and footplates swung away. Leave room for helper.
Helper: Stand to the right of person and grasp the person's right hand in your right hand with a thumb-through grip. Put your left hand under person's arm. Make sure your right foot is pointing across in front of person, and left foot is pointing under chair.
Person: Put left hand on arm-rest of chair.

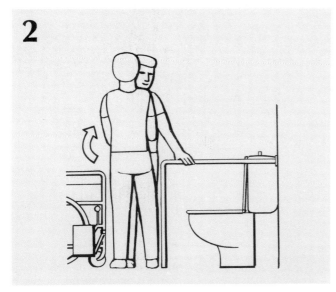

On command '1–2–3–stand'
Person: Push on arm rest and pull on helper's hand to stand up.
Helper: Allow person to take weight on hand and assist person into standing.
Person: Transfer left hand to rail.

Together walk feet around until person's legs are against toilet bowl. Arrange clothing.

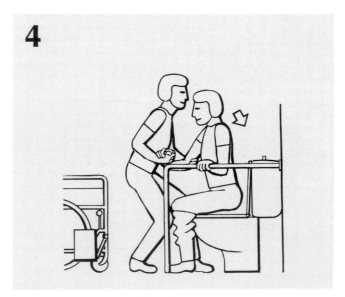

Helper: Lunge toward toilet as person sits down.
Person: Sit down holding onto rail.

NOTE
1. *Because toilet areas are usually small this transfer is shown, but where space permits park chair at a 45° angle to the toilet.*
2. *A rotating board may be useful (see Ch. 3).*

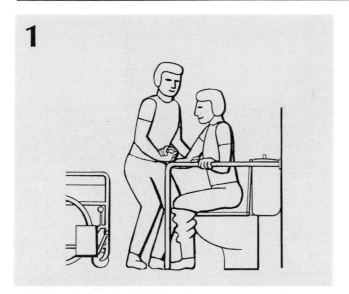

1

Park chair facing toilet, brakes on and footplates swung away. Leave room for helper.
Helper: Stand on right side of person and grasp the person's right hand in your right hand with a thumb-through grip. Put your left hand under person's arm. Make sure your left foot is pointing to the toilet and your right foot is pointing across in front of person.
Person: Put left hand on rail.

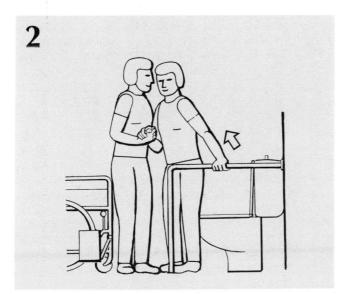

2

On command '1–2–3–stand'
Person: Pull on rail and helper's hand to stand up.
Helper: Allow person to take weight on hand and help person into standing. Arrange clothing.

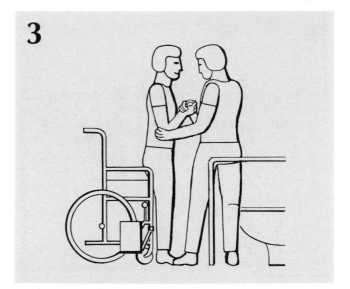

3

Together walk feet around until backs of person's legs are against chair.

4

Helper: Lunge towards chair as person sits down.

NOTE
1. *Because toilet areas are usually small this transfer is shown, but where space permits park the chair at a 45° angle to the toilet.*
2. *A rotating board may be useful (see Ch. 3).*

CHAIR TO TOILET

MUCH ASSISTED
One helper required

1

Park chair facing the toilet, brakes on and footplates swung away. Leave room for helper.
Helper: Help person towards edge of chair. Position your feet and knees so that person's feet and knees are blocked from slipping forward and bending. Hold person in shoulder-blade grip.
Person: Put arms around shoulders of helper.

2

Helper: Squat slightly.
On command '1–2–3–stand'
Helper: Stand up to help person stand.

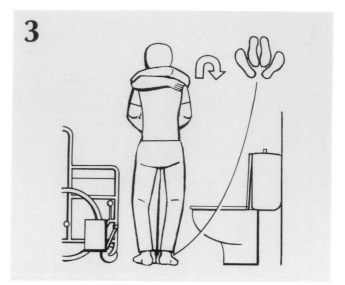

3

When balanced, together pivot slowly around towards toilet making sure knees are prevented from bending.

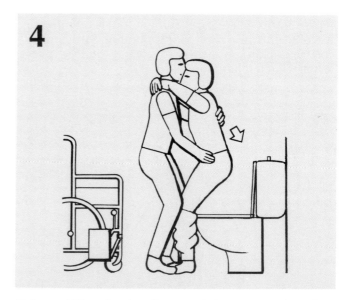

4

Helper: When backs of person's legs are against the toilet bowl, arrange clothing and push on front of person's hip to ensure better sitting position.

NOTE
1. Because toilet areas are usually small this transfer is shown, but where space permits park chair at 45° angle to the toilet.
2. A rotating board may be useful (see Ch. 3).

1

Park chair facing the toilet, brakes on and footplates swung away. Leave room for helper.
Helper: Position feet and knees so that person's feet and knees are blocked from slipping forward or bending. Hold person in a shoulder-blade grip.
Person: Put arms around shoulders of helper.

2

Helper: Squat slightly.
On command '1–2–3–stand'
Helper: Stand up to help person stand. Arrange clothing.

3

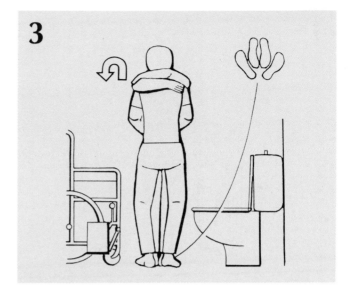

When balanced, together pivot feet around slowly until the backs of person's legs are against the chair seat.

4

Helper: Push on front of person's hip to ensure better sitting position.

NOTE
1. Because toilet areas are usually small this transfer is shown, but where space permits park chair at 45° angle to the toilet.
2. A rotating board may be useful (see Ch. 3).

1

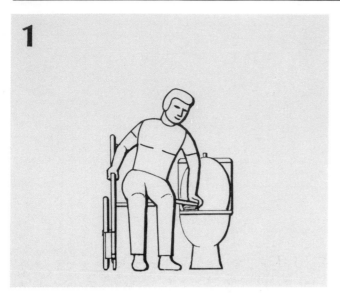

Park chair beside toilet. Remove near side arm-rest. Brakes on and footplates swung away. Place slide board under left buttock and other end on toilet seat. A small damp towel, folded and placed between the slide board and toilet seat, will help prevent slipping.

2

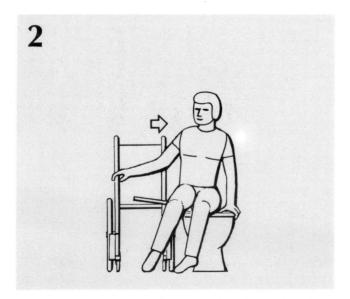

Put left hand on end of slide board and right hand on arm-rest. Push down on hands and slide along board onto toilet.

3

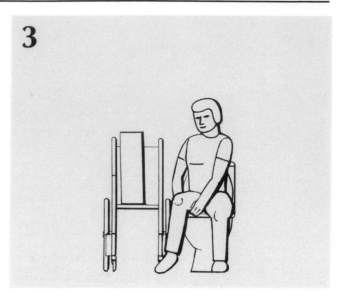

Lift legs across and remove slide board and towel, and arrange clothing.

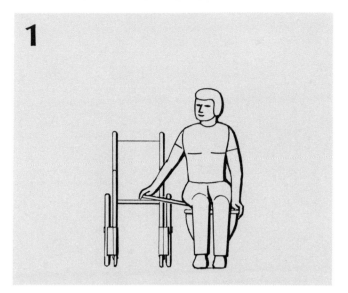

1

Park chair beside toilet. Remove near side arm-rest. Brakes on and footplates swung away. Arrange clothing. Place slide board under right buttock and other end on seat of wheelchair. A small damp towel, folded and placed between slide board and toilet seat, will prevent slipping.

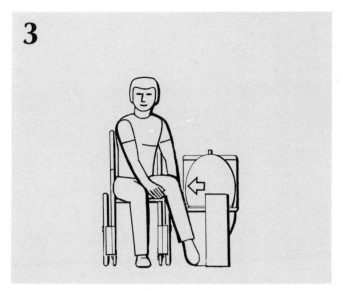

3

Remove slide board and towel, and lift legs across.

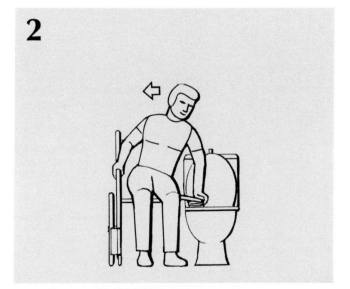

2

Put right hand on end of slide board and left hand on toilet seat. Push down on hands and slide along board onto chair.

UNASSISTED

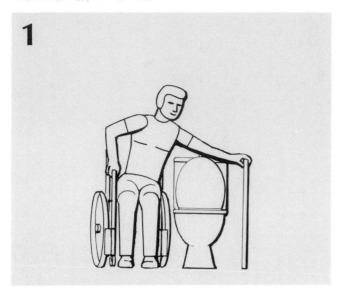

Park chair at a slight angle to toilet. Remove near side arm-rest. Brakes on and footplates swung away. Make sure feet are flat on floor and directly under knees. Reach left hand across to rail and put right hand on arm-rest.

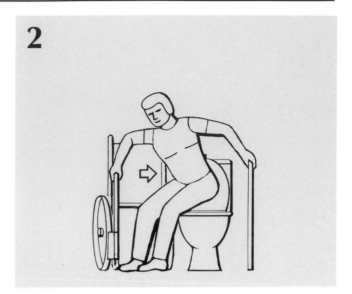

Pull/push on hands and lift buttocks up and over onto toilet. Arrange clothing.

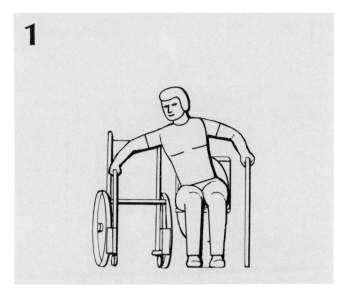

1

Park chair at a slight angle to toilet. Remove near side arm-rest. Brakes on and footplates swung away. Arrange clothing. Make sure feet are flat on floor and directly under knees. Reach right hand to far arm-rest and put left hand on rail or on toilet seat.

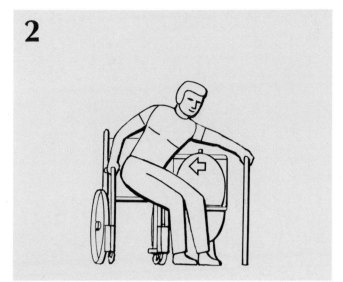

2

Push on hands and lift buttocks up and over onto chair.

CHAIR TO TOILET

MUCH ASSISTED
One helper required

1

Helper: Park chair opposite toilet, brakes on, footplates swung away and arm-rests removed. Rock person from side to side to arrange clothing.

2

Helper: Face person and tuck person's head under your left arm. Hold person's elbows tightly against his body. Place left foot beside person's feet and right foot across the front of person's feet.

3

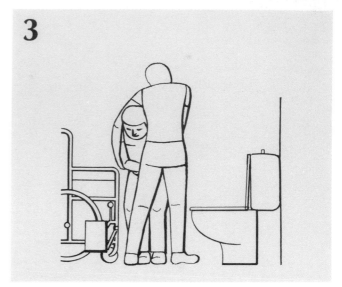

On command '1–2–3–stand'
Helper: Rock weight from left foot to right foot and pivot person around to right.

4

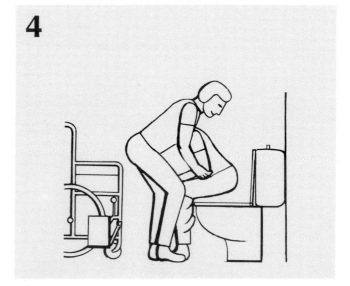

Helper: Help person lower onto toilet.

NOTE
1. *This lift is unsuitable for people who are much heavier or larger than the helper.*
2. *Arrange clothing in chair, not on toilet.*
3. *The transfer from toilet to wheelchair is the reverse of the above manoeuvre.*

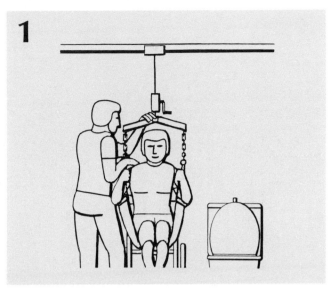

Helper: Park chair next to toilet under the overhead rail. Put on brakes and swing footplates away. Remove near side arm-rest.
Helper: Arrange clothes. Position slings under person. Attach slings to hoist.

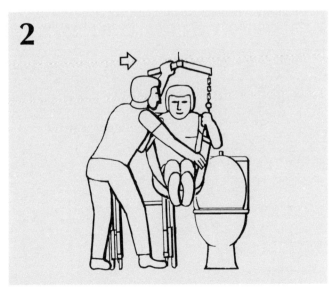

Helper: Elevate person and slide hoist along the track so that person is positioned over the toilet.

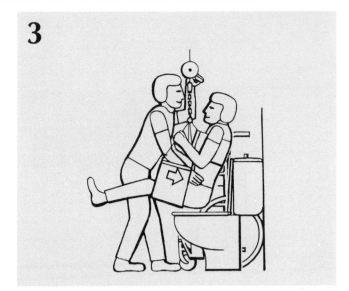

Helper: Lower person onto the toilet. Just before sitting, push on person's knees with your knees to ensure better sitting position.

NOTE
1. *In a narrow toilet the track may be installed so that a 180° turn is needed with the chair facing the toilet.*
2. *Where space permits, a mobile floor hoist may be used.*

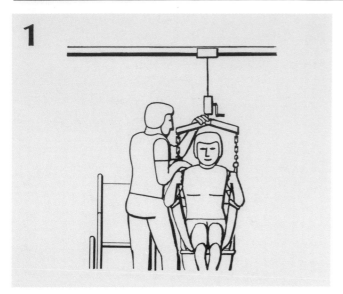

Helper: Park chair next to toilet under overhead rail. Brakes on and footplates swung away. Remove near side arm-rest. Position slings and attach to hoist.

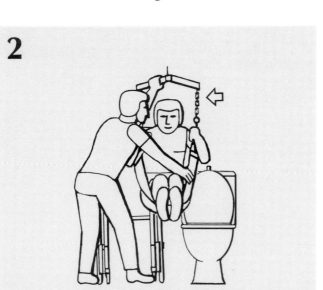

Helper: Elevate person and slide hoist along track so that person is positioned over chair.

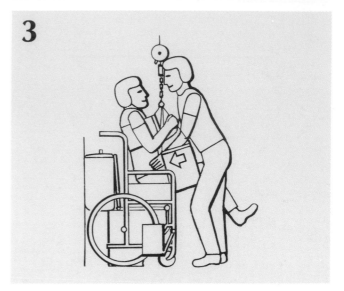

Helper: Lower person into chair. Just before sitting, push on the person's knees with your knees to ensure better sitting position. Arrange clothes.

NOTE
1. *In a narrow toilet the track may be installed so that a 180° turn is needed with the chair facing the toilet.*
2. *Where space permits, a mobile floor hoist may be used.*

Chair/bath transfers

7

When bathing, some people may be able to use a low seat placed in the bath below the water-line. The person lowers down onto this seat after having completed a chair to bath transfer (see p. 86). Alternatively, the person can remain on the high bath seat (see p. 82) and wash with a flannel or hand-held shower.

At all times, the decision as to which method to use is conditional on the ability of the person to get *out* of the bath safely. If the person is too heavy or too disabled, then a mechanical hoist should be used for the transfer (for example, see p. 89). This is to ensure the safety of the helper(s) and the person.

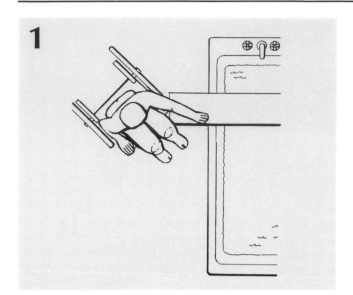

1

Park chair at 45° angle to bath seat. Brakes on, bath side arm-rest removed and footplates swung away. Fill bath. Undress. Put left hand on bath seat and right hand on arm-rest.

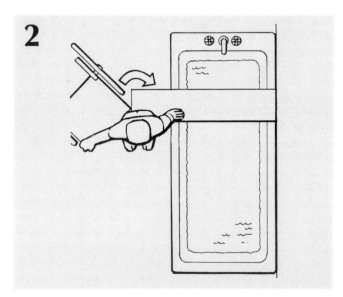

2

Push on hands to stand up. Pivot around slowly until legs are against bath seat. Transfer right hand to end of bath seat before sitting down.

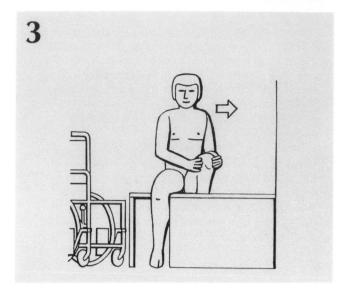

3

Lift legs into bath and move across bath seat to the centre.

NOTE
1. *Be sure of your grip and footing on slippery wet surfaces; use a non-slip mat.*
2. *A rotating board may be useful (see Ch. 3).*

1

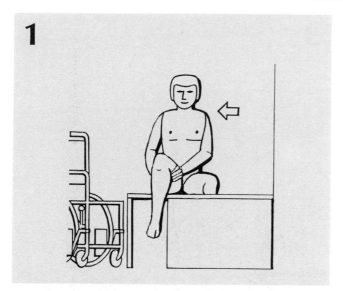

Park chair at 45° angle to bath seat. Brakes on, bath side arm-rest removed and footplates swung away. Empty bath and partly dry self. Move to edge of bath seat and lift legs out of bath. Dry feet well.

2

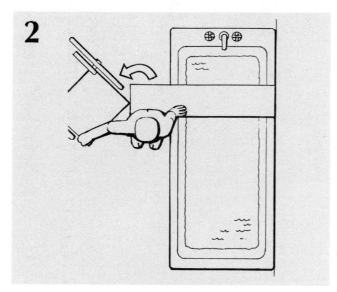

Put right hand on arm-rest and left hand on bath seat. Push on hands to stand up. Pivot around slowly until backs of legs are against chair.

3

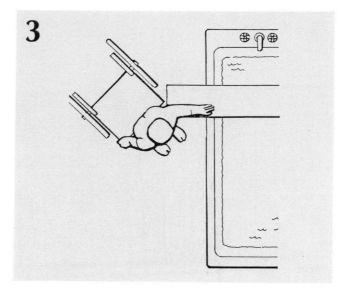

Move left hand to end of bath seat before sitting down. Complete drying.

NOTE
1. Be sure of your grip and footing on slippery wet surfaces; use a non-slip mat.
2. A rotating board may be useful (see Ch. 3).

PARTLY ASSISTED
One helper required

© Tony Pelosi and Margaret Gleeson 1988

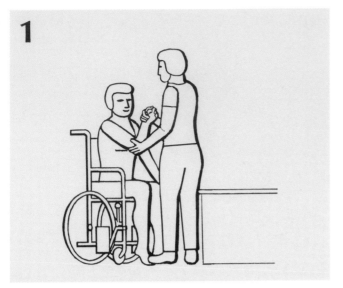

Park chair at 45° angle to bath seat. Brakes on, bath side arm-rest removed and footplates swung away. Fill bath. Undress.
Helper: Take a thumb-through grip with person's right hand and hold person's elbow with your left hand. Point left foot at chair and right foot in direction of movement.
Person: Put left hand on bath seat.

On command '1–2–3–stand'
Helper: Assist person to stand and pivot.
Person: Pull on gripped hand and push on left hand to stand up and pivot slowly around until back of legs are against bath seat before sitting down.

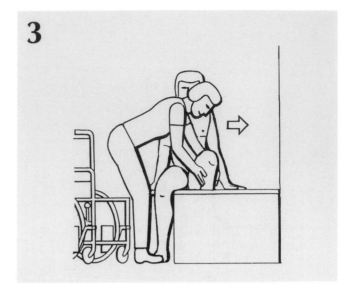

Helper: Assist person to put legs in bath and to move to centre of bath seat.

NOTE
1. *Be sure of your grip and footing on slippery wet surfaces; use a non-slip mat.*
2. *A rotating board may be useful (see Ch. 3).*

Stand pivot

© Tony Pelosi and Margaret Gleeson 1988

1

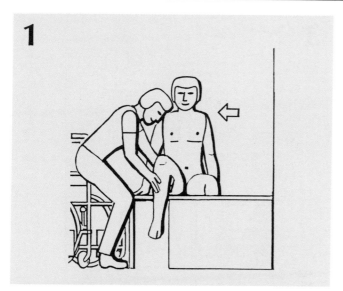

Park chair at 45° angle to bath seat. Brakes on, bath side arm-rest removed and footplates swung away.
Helper: Empty bath and assist in partly drying person. Assist person to move to edge of bath seat and to lift legs out of bath. Dry feet well.

2

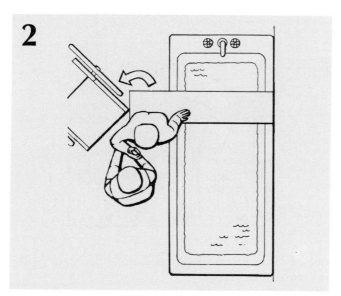

Helper: Take thumb-through grip with person's right hand and hold person's elbow with your left hand. Point left foot at chair and right foot at bath seat.
Person: Put left hand on bath seat.
On command '1–2–3–stand'
Helper: Assist person to stand and pivot.
Person: Pull on gripped hand and push on bath seat to stand up and pivot slowly around until backs of legs are against chair.

3

Helper: Maintain hand grips to assist person to sit down.
Person: Transfer left hand to seat of chair before sitting down.

NOTE
1. *Be sure of your grip and footing on slippery wet surfaces; use a non-slip mat.*
2. *A rotating board may be useful (see Ch. 3).*

1

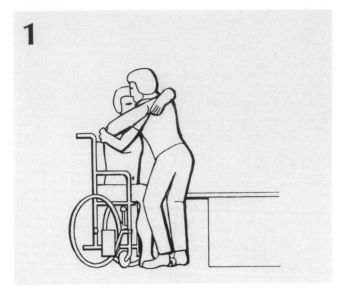

Park chair at 45° angle to bath seat. Brakes on, bath side arm-rest removed and footplates swung away.
Helper: Fill bath and assist person to undress. Take person in a shoulder-blade grip and position your feet and knees so that person's feet and knees are blocked from slipping.
Person: Put arms around shoulders of helper.

2

Helper: Squat slightly.
On command '1–2–3–stand'
Helper: Stand up to assist person to stand.
Person: Keep head bent forward and grip on shoulders of helper to stand up.

3

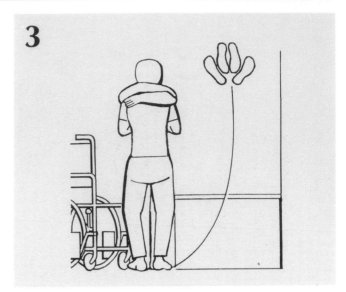

Together pivot slowly around. Ensure that person's legs are against bath seat before sitting down.

4

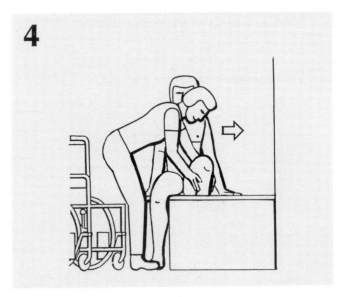

Helper: Lift person's legs into bath and help person to centre of bath seat.

NOTE
1. *Be sure of your grip and footing on slippery wet surfaces; use a non-slip mat.*
2. *A rotating board may be useful (see Ch. 3).*

© Tony Pelosi and Margaret Gleeson 1988

1

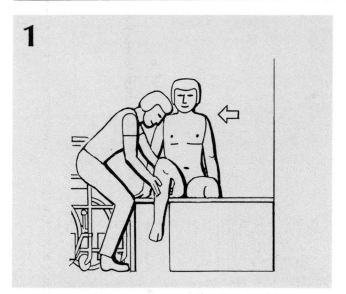

Park chair at 45° angle to bath seat. Brakes on, bath side arm-rest removed and footplates swung away.
Helper: Empty bath and assist person to partly dry self. Assist person to move to edge of bath seat. Lift person's legs out of bath. Dry feet well.

2

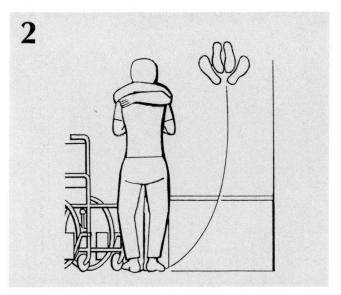

Helper: Take person in a shoulder-blade grip and position your feet and knees so that person's feet and knees are blocked from slipping. Squat slightly.
Person: Put arms around shoulder of helper.
On command '1–2–3–stand'.
Helper: Stand up to assist person to stand.
Person: Keep head bent forward and grip on shoulders of helper to stand up.

3

Together pivot slowly around. Ensure that person's legs are against the chair before sitting down.

Helper: Assist person to finish drying self.

NOTE
1. *Be sure of your grip and footing on slippery wet surfaces; use a non-slip mat.*
2. *A rotating board may be useful (see Ch. 3).*

1

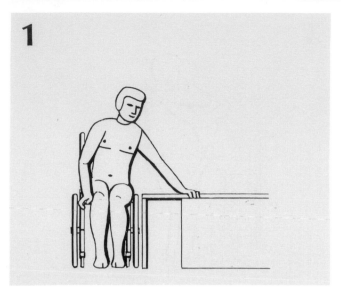

Park chair beside bath seat. Brakes on, bath side arm-rest removed, and footplates swung away. Fill bath. Undress. Put left hand on bath seat and right hand on seat of chair. Push down on hands to raise bottom over onto bath seat.

2

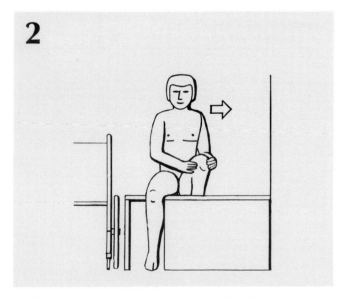

Lift legs into bath. Move to centre of bath seat.

3

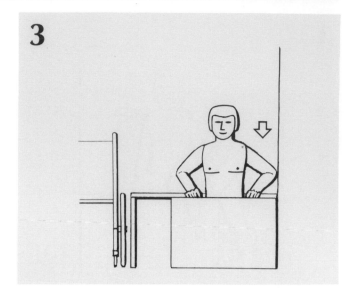

If necessary, put hands on bath seat and lower buttocks onto a lower seat or into bath (see p. 79).

NOTE
Be sure of your grip on slippery wet surfaces; use a non-slip mat.

1

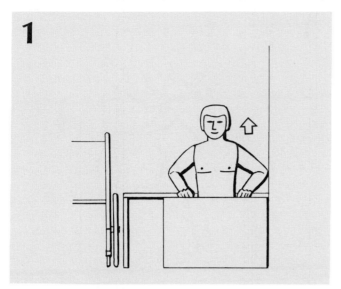

Chair parked beside bath seat. Brakes on, bath side arm-rest removed, and footplates swung away. If sitting in bath or on lower seat, put hands on upper bath seat and lift buttocks up onto bath seat. Empty bath and partly dry self.

2

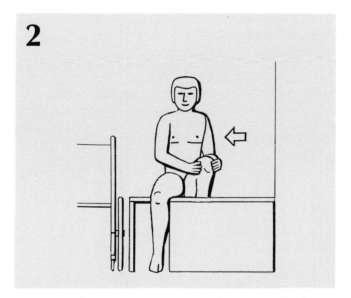

Move to edge of bath seat and lift legs out of bath. Dry feet well.

3

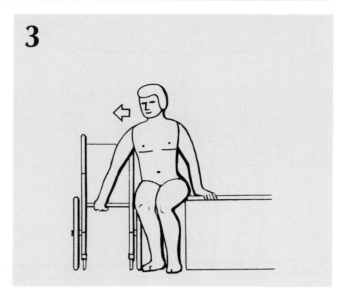

Put right hand on seat of chair and left hand on bath seat. Push down on hands to raise buttocks over into chair. Finish drying self.

NOTE
Be sure of your grip on slippery wet surfaces; use a non-slip mat.

CHAIR TO BATH

MUCH ASSISTED
One helper required

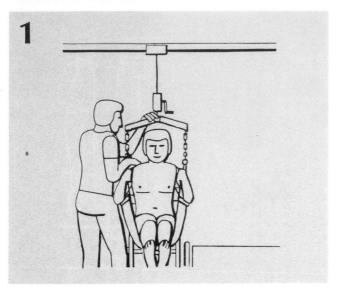

Park chair alongside bath underneath overhead rail. Brakes on, bath side arm-rest removed and footplates swung away. Fill bath and undress person. Position slings under person and attach to hoist.

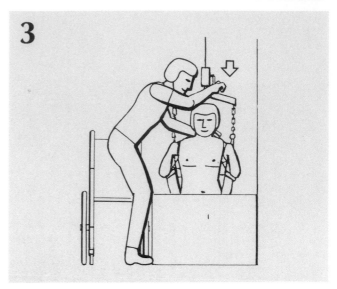

Lower person into bath making sure head is supported as person reaches the bottom. Remove slings.

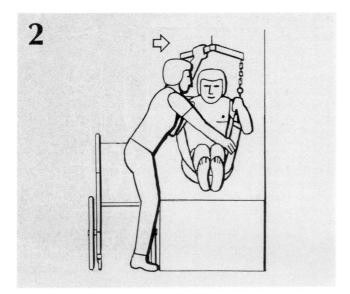

Crank hoist until person is clear of chair. Slide hoist along track so that person is over water.

1

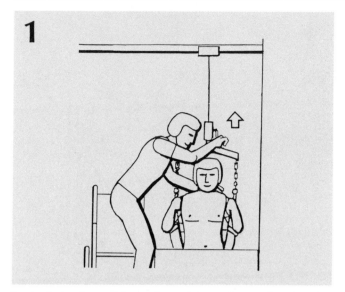

Park chair alongside bath underneath overhead rail. Brakes on, bath side arm-rest removed and footplates swung away. Empty bath and dry person as much as possible. Position slings under person and attach to hoist.

3

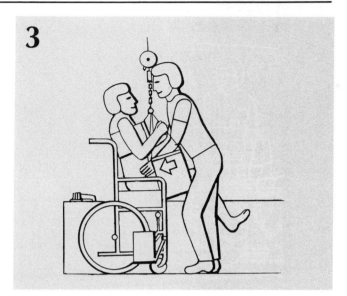

Lower person down. Just before sitting, push forward on person's hip to make sure of better sitting position. Remove slings. Finish drying and dress person.

2

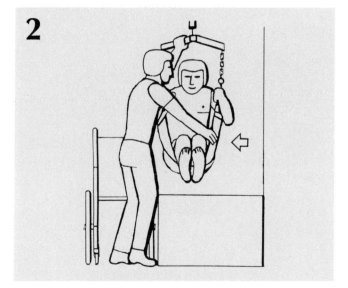

Crank hoist until person is clear of bath. Slide hoist along track until person is above chair.

1

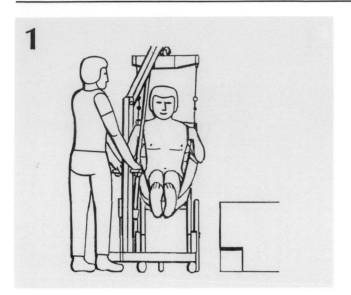

Park chair near bath. Brakes on, bath side arm-rest removed and footplates swung away. Fill bath. Undress person. Position slings under person and attach to hoist.

2

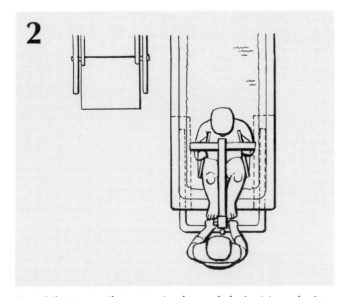

Crank hoist until person is clear of chair. Move hoist so that person is above water. Put brakes on.

3

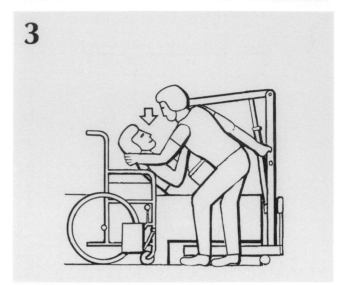

Lower person into bath, being sure to support head as person reaches bottom. Remove slings.

NOTE
This hoist can be used only if the bath is designed to accommodate its horizontal legs.

1

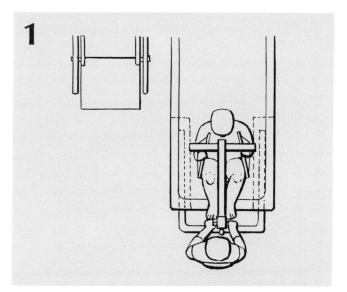

Park chair near bath. Brakes on, bath side arm-rest removed and footplates swung away. Empty bath and dry person as much as possible. Position slings under person and attach to hoist.

3

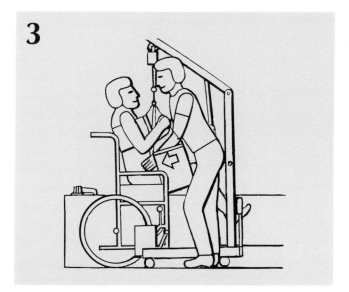

Lower person into chair. Just before sitting, push forward on person's hip to obtain better sitting position. Remove slings. Finish drying and dress person.

NOTE
This hoist can be used only if the bath is designed to accommodate its horizontal legs.

2

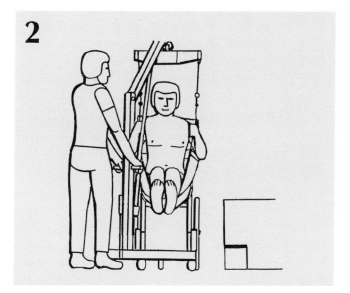

Crank hoist until person is clear of bath. Move hoist so that person is above chair. Put brakes on.

Chair/car transfers

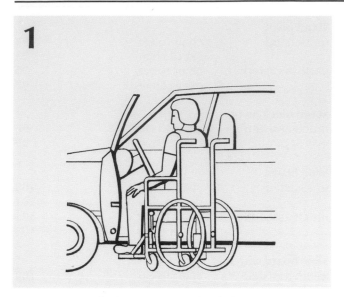

1

Remove car side footplate, put both feet on remaining footplate and park chair as close to car as possible and at a slight angle to car. Put brakes on, remove car side arm-rest. Wind window down.

3

Pivot on feet so that backs of legs are against car. Bend head forward and sit down on car seat.

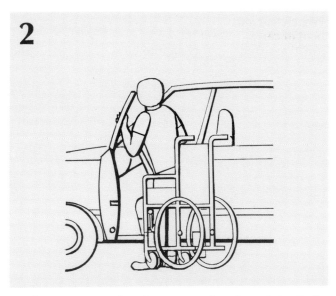

2

Put feet on ground and remove other footplate. Pull on windscreen pillar and door edge to stand up.

4

Lift legs into car.

NOTE
1. *Transfer is easier if car and wheelchair are on the same street level.*
2. *Opening window gives a useful emergency grip area.*
3. *It is assumed that some help is available to remove wheelchair.*
4. *A rotating board may be useful (see Ch. 3).*

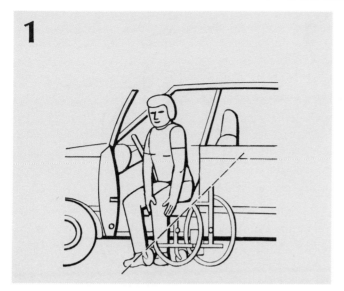

Remove car side footplate and arm-rest. Park chair as close as possible to car at a slight angle. Put brakes on. Put feet on ground and move toward edge of seat. Wind window down.

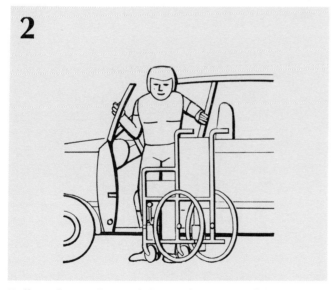

Pull on door pillar and door edge to stand up.

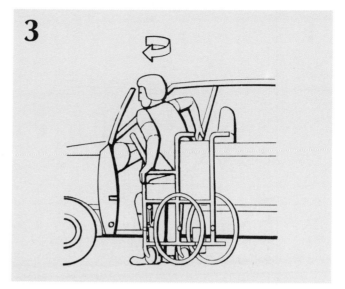

Transfer grip from door pillar to far arm-rest and other hand to door pillar. Pivot around until legs are against chair before sitting.

NOTE
1. *Transfer is easier if car and chair are on same street level.*
2. *Opening window gives a useful emergency grip area.*
3. *It is assumed that some help is available to position the chair.*
4. *A rotating board may be useful (see Ch. 3).*

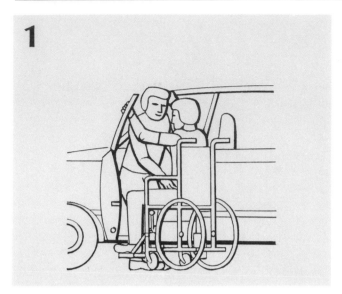

Helper: Remove car side footplate and arm-rest. Park chair as close as possible to car and at a slight angle (leave room for helper). Put brakes on. Wind window down.
Person: Hold onto windscreen pillar and door edge.
Helper: Hold waistband of person.

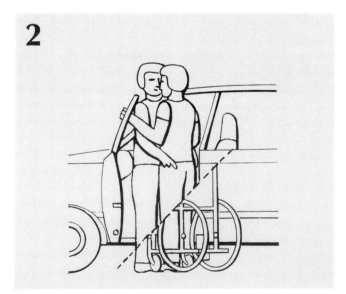

On command '1–2–3–stand'
Person: Pull on hand holds to stand up.
Helper: Assist by pulling on person's waistband.

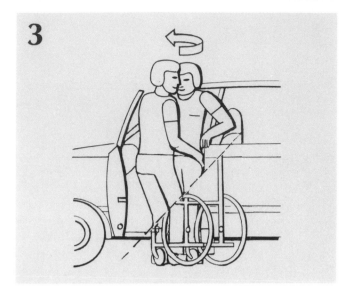

Person: Pivot on feet until backs of legs are against car. Transfer left hand to door pillar. Bend head forward and sit down on car seat.

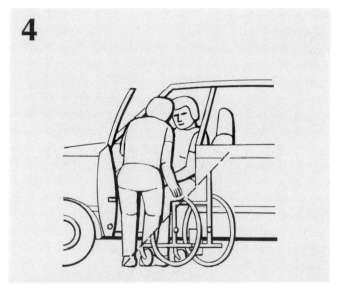

Helper: Assist person to put feet in car.

NOTE
1. It is important to make sure person has head bent forward in this manoeuvre.
2. Transfer is easier if car and wheelchair are on same street level.
3. Opening window gives an emergency grip area.
4. A rotating board may be useful (see Ch. 3).

© Tony Pelosi and Margaret Gleeson 1988

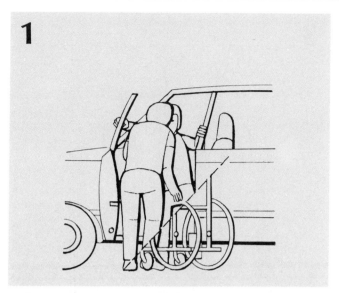

Helper: Remove car side footplate and arm-rest. Park chair as close as possible to car at a slight angle (leave room for helper). Put brakes on. Wind window down.
Helper: Assist person to put feet on ground.
Person: Move forward towards edge of seat. Keep head bent forward. Hold onto door edge and door pillar.

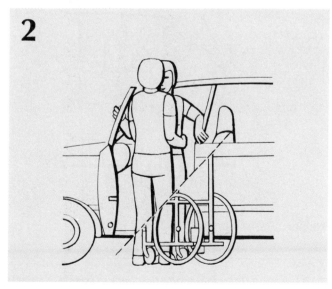

Helper: Squat slightly.
On command '1–2–3–stand'
Person: Pull on hand holds and stand up.
Helper: Hold onto waistband, stand up by straightening knees.

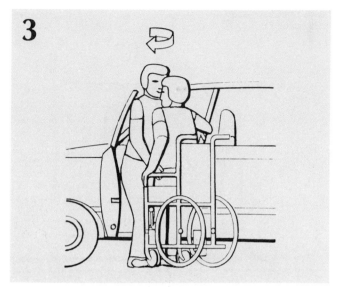

Person: Pivot around until backs of legs are against chair. Swap left hand to arm of chair and right hand to door pillar. Use these supports to sit down.
Helper: As person sits, push gently at front of hip to ensure better sitting position.

NOTE
1. *Transfer is easier if car and wheelchair are on same street level.*
2. *Opening window gives an emergency grip area.*
3. *A rotating board may be useful (see Ch. 3).*

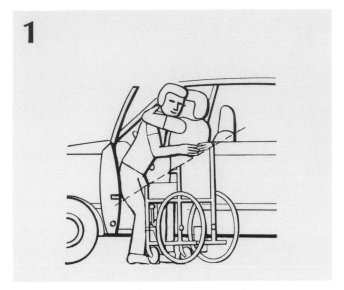

Helper: Remove car side footplate and arm-rest. Park chair as close as possible to car and at a slight angle (leave room for helper). Put brakes on. Wind window down.
Person: Put arms around shoulders of helper. Keep head bent forward.
Helper: Hold person in shoulder-blade grip and block feet and knees with your feet and knees.

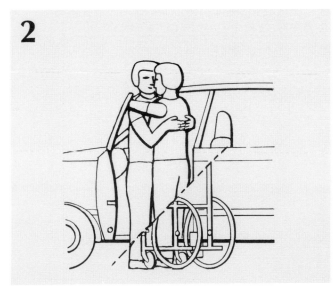

Helper: Squat slightly.
On command '1–2–3–stand'
Helper: Stand up to help person to stand.

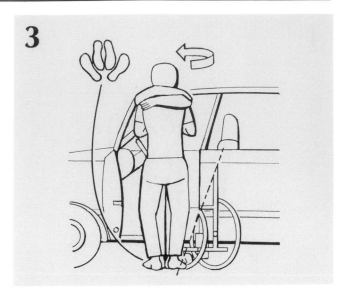

Helper: Pivot around until backs of person's legs are against car. Bend person's head forward and help sit on car seat.

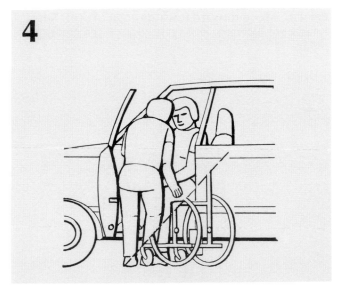

Helper: Assist person to put feet in car.

NOTE
1. *It is important to make sure that person has head bent forward in this manoeuvre.*
2. *Transfer is easier if car and wheelchair are on same street level.*
3. *Opening window gives an emergency grip area.*
4. *A rotating board may be useful (see Ch. 3).*

1

Helper: Remove car side footplate and arm-rest. Park chair as close as possible to car at a slight angle (leave room for helper). Put brakes on. Wind window down.

2

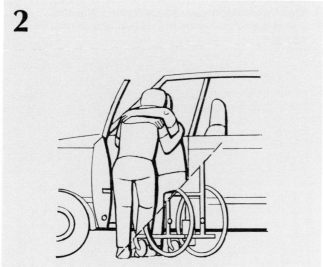

Helper: Assist person to put feet on ground and to move forward towards edge of seat.
Person: Keep head bent forward.
Helper: Hold person in shoulder-blade grip and block feet and knees with your feet and knees.
Person: Put arms around shoulders of helper.

3

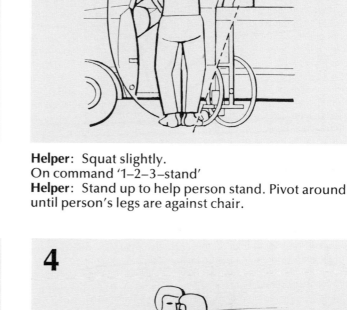

Helper: Squat slightly.
On command '1–2–3–stand'
Helper: Stand up to help person stand. Pivot around until person's legs are against chair.

4

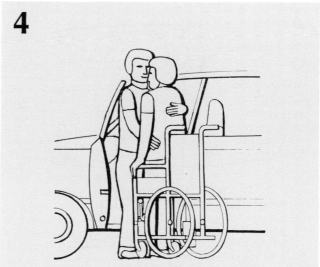

Helper: As person sits, push gently at front of hip to ensure better sitting position.

NOTE
1. _It is important to make sure that person has head bent forward in this manoeuvre._
2. _Transfer is easier if car and wheelchair are on same street level._
3. _Opening window gives an emergency grip area._
4. _A rotating board may be useful (see Ch. 3)._

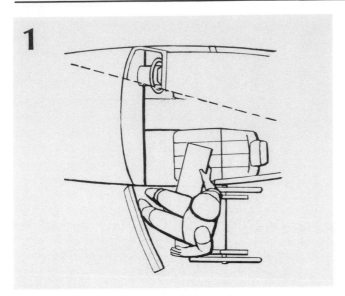

1

Remove car side arm-rest and footplate. Park chair as close to car as possible. Brakes on. Position slide board under buttock and on car seat. Wind window down.

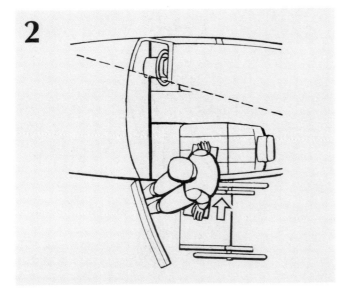

3

Lift legs into car and remove board.

NOTE
1. Keep head bent forward throughout manoeuvre.
2. Transfer is easier if car and wheelchair are on same street level.
3. Opening window gives an emergency grip area.
4. It is assumed that some help is available to remove chair.

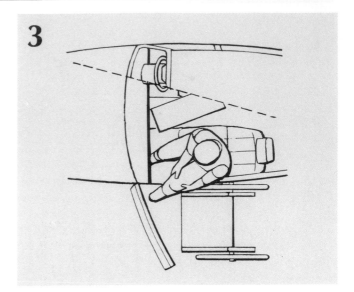

2

Bend head forward. Press down on end of board with one hand and on seat of chair with other hand. Slide along board onto car seat.

1

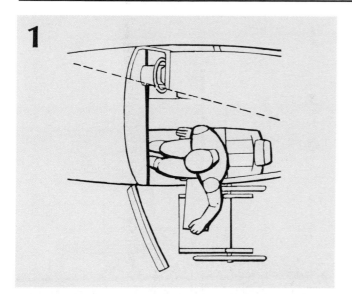

Park chair as close as possible to car, with car side arm-rest and footplate removed. Brakes on. Wind window down. Position slide board under buttock and on chair.

2

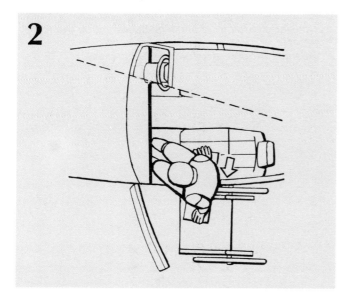

Bend head forward. Push down on end of board and on car seat. Slide across board onto chair.

3

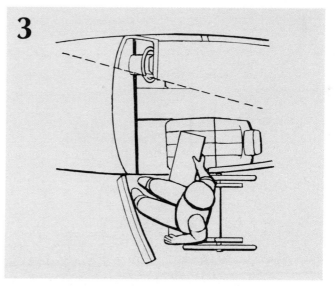

Lift legs out of car. Remove board and replace arm-rest and footplate.

NOTE
1. *Keep head bent forward throughout manoeuvre.*
2. *Transfer is easier if car and wheelchair are on same street level.*
3. *Opening window gives an emergency grip area.*
4. *It is assumed that some help is available to position chair.*

MUCH ASSISTED
One helper required

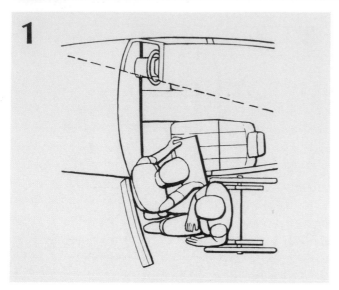

Helper: Remove car side arm-rest and footplate. Park chair as close to car as possible (leave room for helper). Brakes on. Wind window down. Position slideboard under buttock of person and on car seat.

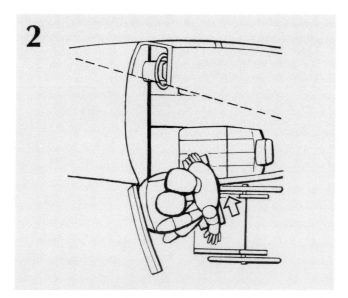

Person: Bend head forward. Press one hand on end of board and other hand on seat of chair.
Helper: Hold at person's hips.
On command '1–2–3–slide'
Person: Slide along board taking as much weight as possible on hands.
Helper: Assist person to slide along board.

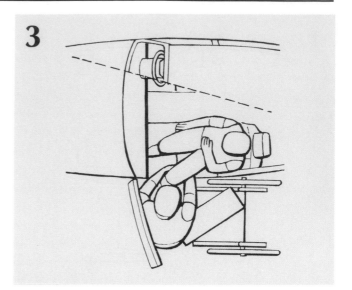

Helper: Remove chair, lift person's legs into car and remove board.

NOTE
1. *Person needs to keep head bent forward throughout the manoeuvre.*
2. *Transfer is easier if car and wheelchair are on the same street level.*
3. *Opening window gives emergency grip area.*

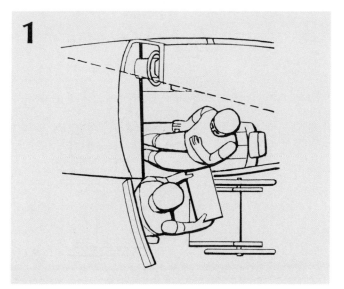

1

Helper: Park chair as close as possible to car (leave room for helper). Brakes on and car side arm-rest removed. Position board under person's buttock and on seat of wheelchair. Wind window down.

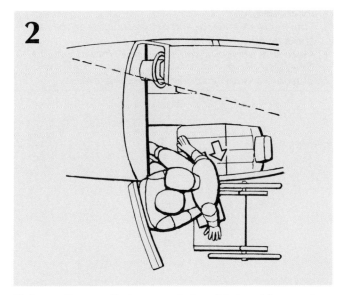

2

Helper: Ensure that person's head is bent forward. Grip person's waistband and slide person along board onto seat of chair.

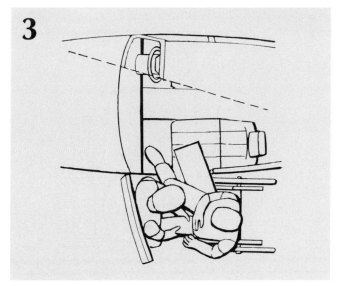

3

Helper: Lift person's legs out of car and put feet on footplate. Remove board. Adjust sitting position.

NOTE
1. *Person needs to keep head bent forward throughout manoeuvre.*
2. *Transfer is easier if car and wheelchair are on same street level.*
3. *Opening window gives emergency grip area.*

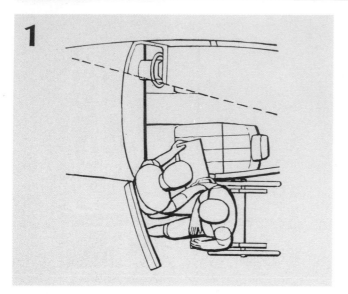

Helper: Remove car side footplate and arm-rest. Park chair as close as possible to car and at a slight angle (leave room for helper). Brakes on. Wind window down.

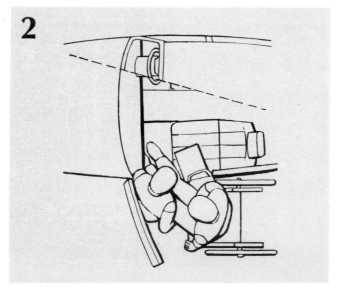

Helper: Move to other side of car. Pull on mat handle to slide person into car.

NOTE
1. *Person needs to keep head bent forward throughout manoeuvre.*
2. *Transfer is easier if car and wheelchair are on the same street level.*
3. *Make sure person is well balanced before moving to other side of car.*
4. *Opening window gives emergency grip area.*

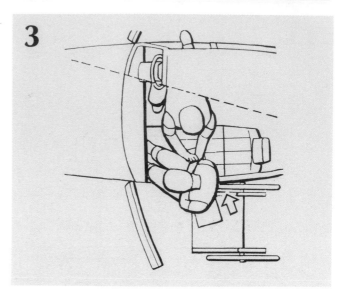

Helper: Position slide board under mat and buttock and other end on car seat. Put person's feet in car. Ensure that person's head is bent forward.

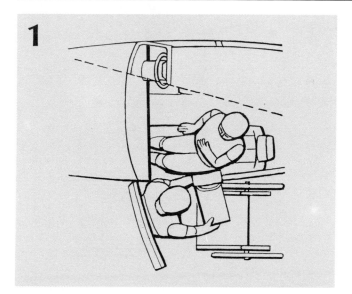

1

Helper: Park chair as close as possible to car with car side footplate and arm-rest removed (leave room for helper). Brakes on. Wind window down.
Helper: Position board under mat and buttock and on seat of chair.

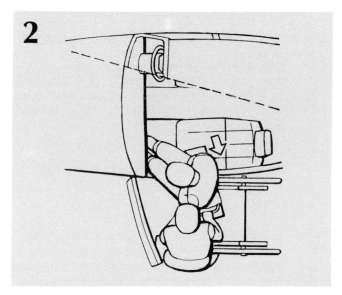

3

Helper: Lift person's feet out of car. Remove board.

NOTE
1. *Person needs to keep head bent forward throughout manoeuvre.*
2. *Transfer is easier if car and wheelchair are on the same street level.*
3. *Opening window gives emergency grip area.*

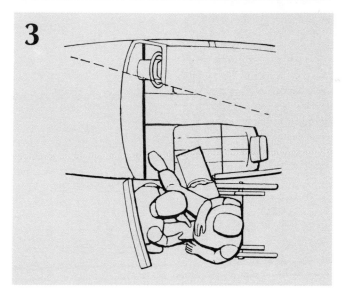

2

Helper: Ensure that person's head is bent forward. Pull on mat handle to slide person along board onto chair.

© Tony Pelosi and Margaret Gleeson 1988

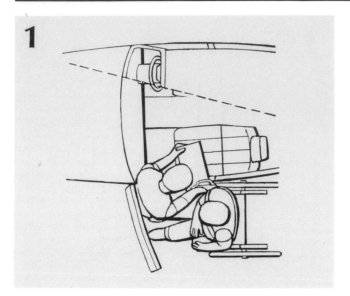

Helper: Park chair as close as possible to car (leave room for helper). Remove car side footplate and arm-rest. Put brakes on. Wind window down.

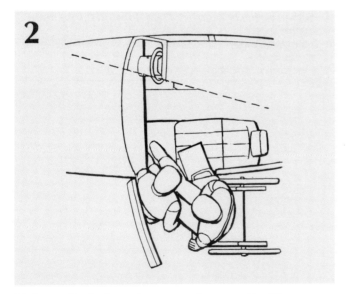

Helper: Move to other side of car. Pull on belt and mat to slide person into car. Remove board.

NOTE
1. *Person needs to keep head bent forward throughout manoeuvre.*
2. *Transfer is easier if car and chair are on the same street level.*
3. *Make sure person is balanced before moving to other side of car.*
4. *Opening window gives emergency grip area.*

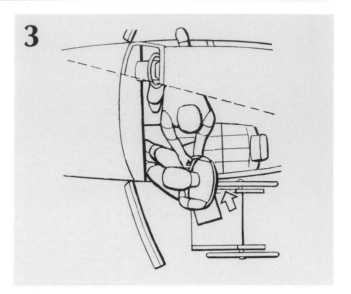

Helper: Put belt under person's arms. Position board under mat and buttock, with other end on car seat. Put person's feet in car. Ensure that person's head is bent forward.

Slide board with mat and belt

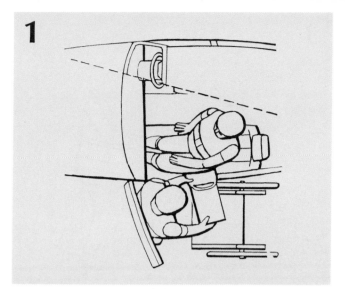

1

Helper: Park chair as close as possible to car with car side footplate and arm-rest removed (leave room for helper). Brakes on. Wind window down.
Helper: Put belt under person's arms. Position board under mat and buttock, with other end on seat of chair. Ensure that person's head is bent forward.

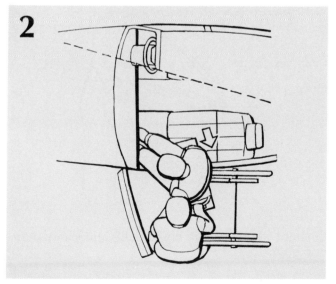

2

Helper: Pull on belt and mat to slide person along board onto chair.

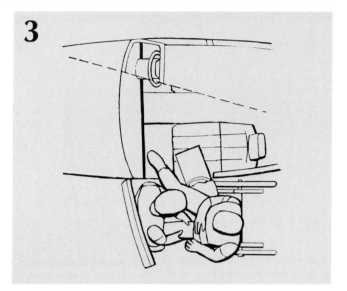

3

Helper: Lift person's legs out of car.

NOTE
1. *Person needs to keep head bent forward throughout manoeuvre.*
2. *Transfer is easier if car and wheelchair are on the same street level.*
3. *Opening window gives emergency grip area.*

MUCH ASSISTED
One helper required

1

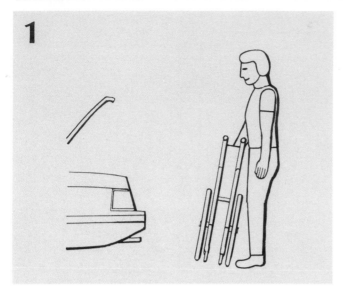

Stand folded wheelchair parallel to boot, at a distance from car which will allow chair to be tipped into horizontal position. Stand close to chair and tilt it to lean against you.

2

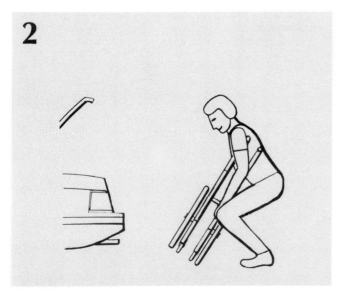

Bend knees, tuck wheelchair handles under left arm and hold them there firmly. Grip wheelchair frame on both sides, with right hand well forward on frame.

3

At the same time as lifting chair with hands, push left knee forwards into chair to pivot it upwards onto edge of boot.

4

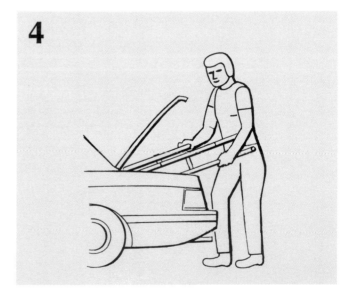

On boot edge, tip chair horizontally and manoeuvre into boot.

NOTE
1. Make the chair light and compact by removing as many parts as possible (e.g. footplates, arm-rests).
2. A rug over the edge of the boot will protect the car and also help slide the chair in.
3. To remove chair from boot reverse the above.

Recreation transfers

Transfer techniques for some limited recreational activities are described in this chapter. It is recognized that there are many other recreational pursuits in which transfers are necessary, but in many instances use can be made of the techniques shown in other chapters in this manual. For example, Chair/car; Chair/floor.

This section is included to show that a wide range of physically demanding recreation is possible for people with disabilities.

MUCH ASSISTED
Three helpers required

Helper 1: Stand at head of horse facing horse. Hold cheek straps.
Helper 2: Stand at off side of horse next to girth.
Helper 3: Position chair at slight angle near the saddle area. Brakes on and foot plates removed.

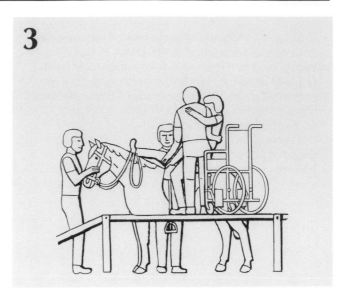

Helper 3: Put right arm behind person's waist. Help lift right leg over horse's neck till person is seated in saddle.
Person: Put left arm around shoulders of helper and right hand on back of saddle.

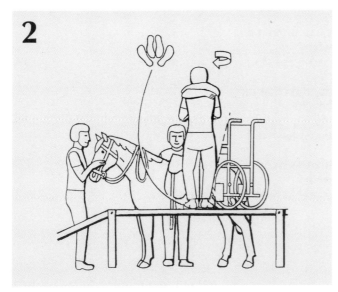

Person: Put arms around shoulders of third helper.
Helper 3: Using a stand block pivot (see p. 45), assist person to stand and pivot towards horse.

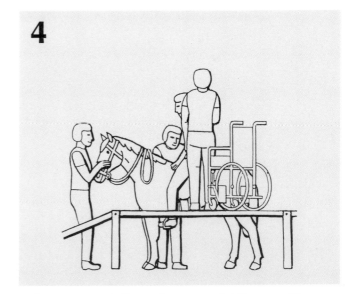

Helpers 2 & 3: Adjust stirrups and sitting position.

MOUNTING HORSE, FROM PLATFORM

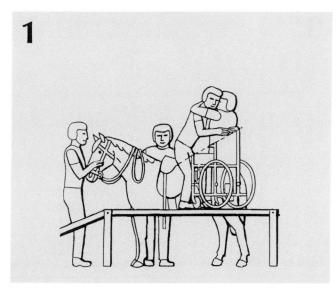

Helper 1: Stand at head of horse facing horse. Hold cheek straps.
Helper 2: Stand at off side of horse next to girth.
Helper 3: Position chair at slight angle near saddle area. Brakes on and footplates removed.

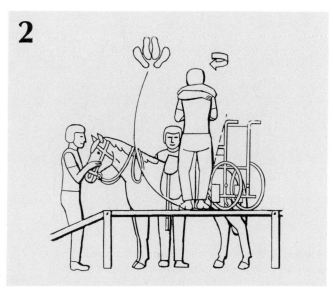

Person: Put arms around shoulders of third helper.
Helper 3: Using a stand block pivot (see p.45), assist person to stand, pivot, and sit against saddle.

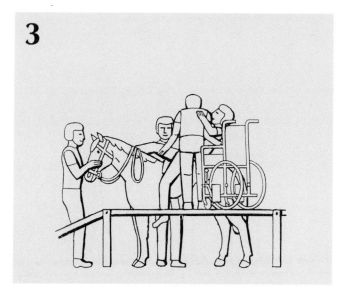

Helper 3: Put right arm behind person's waist. Allow person to lie back towards horse's rump, levering legs up so that right leg can be put across horse's neck.

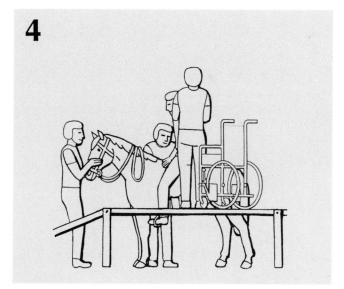

Helpers 2 & 3: Assist person to sit on saddle and adjust stirrups.

DISMOUNTING HORSE, TO PLATFORM

MUCH ASSISTED
Three helpers required

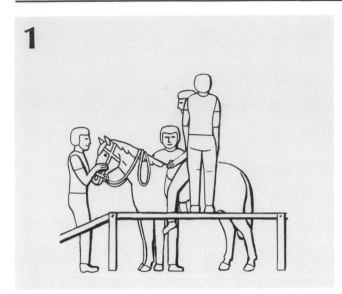

Helper 1: Stand at head of horse facing horse. Hold cheek straps.
Helper 2: Stand at off side of horse at girth.
Helpers 2 & 3: Make sure person's feet are out of stirrups.

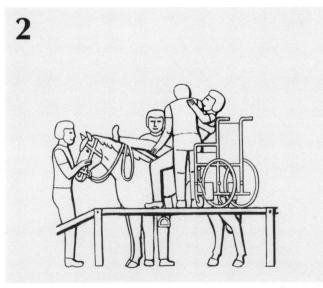

Helper 2: Help lift person's right leg up.
Helper 3: Position chair at slight angle near saddle area. Brakes on, footplates removed. Allow person to lie back in saddle. Support behind back. Lift person's right leg over neck of horse and pivot person around to face you.

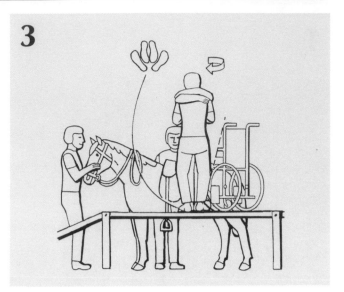

Helper 3: Using a stand block pivot (see p. 45), assist person to stand and pivot towards chair.

Helper 3: When person's legs are against chair, push on person's hip to ensure proper seating position.

DISMOUNTING HORSE, TO GROUND
MUCH ASSISTED
Three helpers required

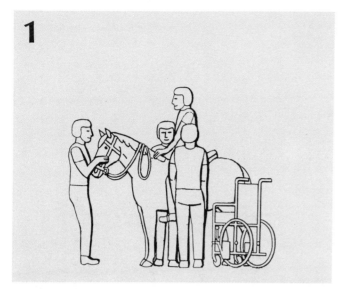

1

Helper 1: Stand at head of horse facing horse. Hold cheek straps.
Helper 2: Stand at off side of horse at girth.
Helper 3: Position chair near horse. Brakes on and footplates removed.

3

Helper 2: Lift person's right leg up over rump of horse.
Helper 3: Receive leg across rump and support person's weight as he descends to ground.
Person: Hold onto front of saddle.

2

Helpers 2 & 3: Assist person to lie forward towards neck of horse. Feet out of stirrups.

4

Person: Steady yourself by holding onto saddle.
Helper 2: Position chair behind person.
Helper 3: Steady person until sitting down.

1

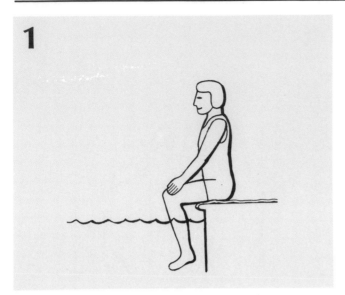

Place mat at pool edge towards deep end at chest depth. Sit on mat with legs over edge.

3

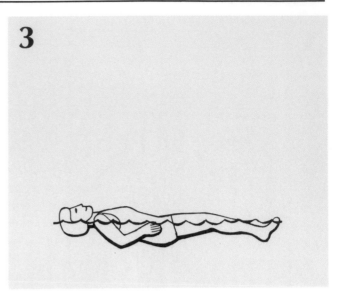

Roll into floating position.

2

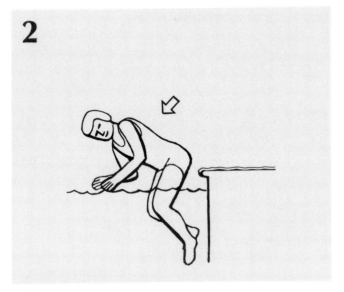

Fall into water.

NOTE
Water should be deep enough to dive.

SWIMMING POOL ENTRY
PARTLY ASSISTED
One helper required

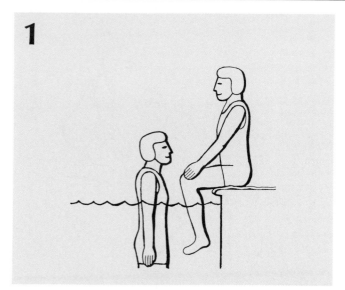

Helper: Place mat at pool edge towards deep end at chest depth.

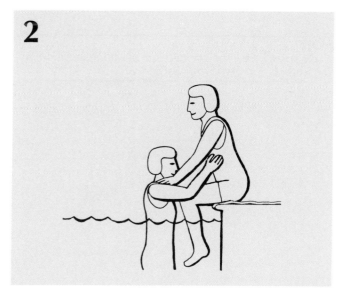

Helper: Stand in water facing person. Hold person's rib-cage.
Person: Sit on mat with legs over edge and place hands on helper's shoulders.

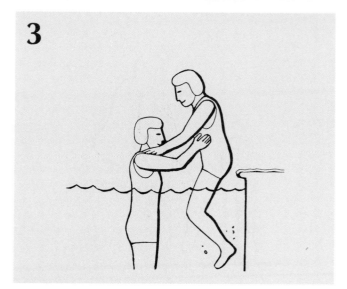

On command '1–2–3–jump'
Person: Lean forward into water.
Helper: Step back and bend knees as person enters water.

MUCH ASSISTED
Two helper required

1

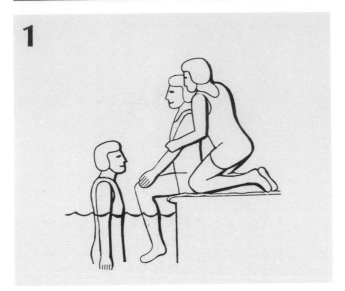

Helper 1: Place mat at pool edge towards deep end at chest depth. Assist person to sit on mat with legs over edge.

3

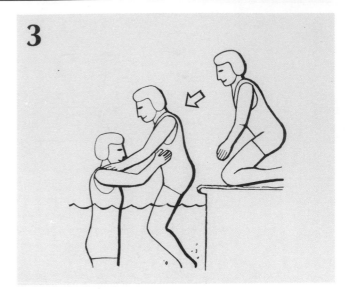

On command '1–2–3–jump'
Person: Lean forward into water.
Helper 2: Support person at rib-cage and help to roll over onto back in a floating position.

NOTE
Make sure person has attained safe breathing position in the water before removing assistance.

2

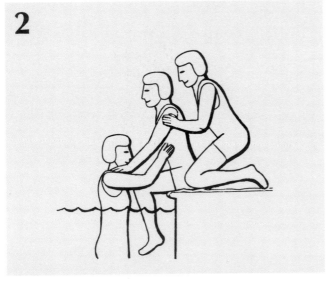

Helper 2: Stand in water facing person. Place hands on person's rib-cage.
Person: Put hands on second helper's shoulders.

1

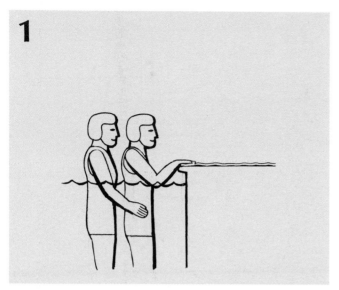

Helper: Place mat at pool edge towards deep end at chest depth.

2

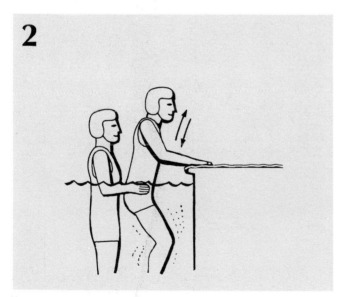

Person: Face edge of pool in line with mat. Place hands up on edge.
Helper: Stand in water behind person with hands at person's hips.

3

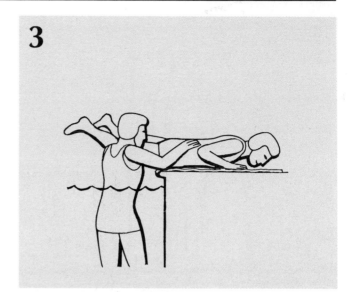

On command '1–2–3–jump'
Person: Make use of buoyancy to progressively jump higher and on 'jump' get upper body onto mat. Use arms to break fall.
Helper: On 'jump' push person out of water and roll person onto side.

SWIMMING POOL EXIT

MUCH ASSISTED
Two helpers required

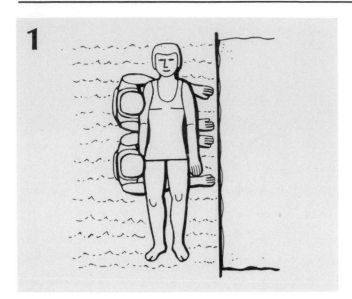

1

Helper: Place mat at pool edge towards deep end at chest depth.
Helper 1: Stand alongside person's chest with left arm under person's neck and shoulder, and right arm under chest. Palms down.
Helper 2: Stand alongside person's hips with left arm under person's low back, and right arm under person's thighs. Palms down.

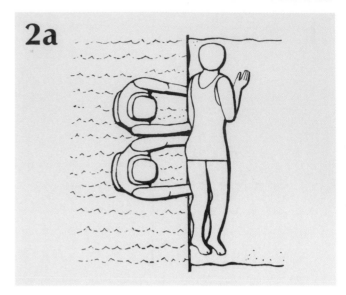

2a

NOTE
With a very large person a third helper is required.

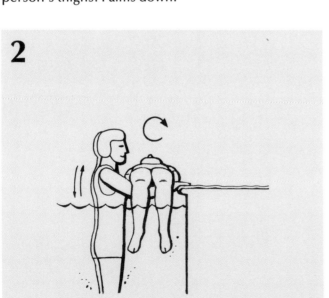

2

On command '1–2–3–lift'
Helpers: Use buoyancy to help person out of water onto mat by placing hands on mat and rolling person down arms onto mat.
Person: Keep head bent forward.

© Tony Pelosi and Margaret Gleeson 1988

1

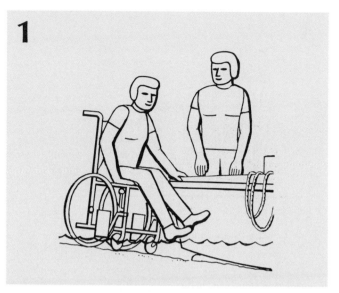

Helper: Steady boat as close to shore as possible.
Person: Park chair close to boat at a slight angle.
Brakes on, arm-rests removed.

2

Person: Lift legs over side of boat and take a firm grip with left hand on boat and right hand on seat of chair.

3

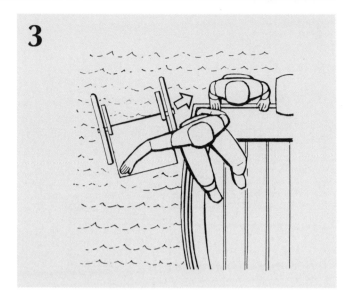

Person: Hitch buttocks up and over onto boat.

NOTE
It is best to reserve an old chair for this activity.

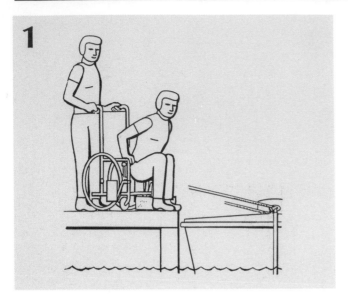

Helper: Securely moor boat in such a way as to prevent ropes hindering access. Position cushion on wharf. Steady chair.
Person: Lower down onto cushion by pressing on seat of chair.

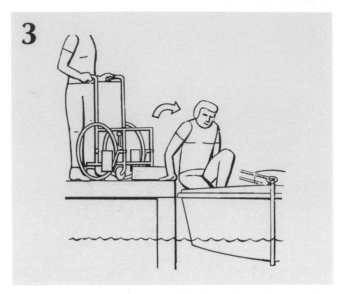

Person: Take a firm grip with left hand on boat and right hand on wharf. Hitch buttocks up and over into boat.

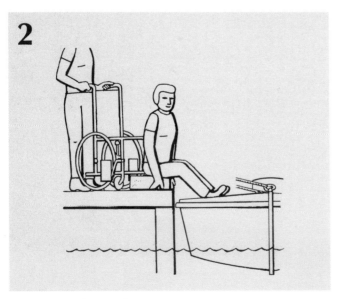

Person: Put legs in boat.

1

Helper: Park chair as close to boat as possible and at a slight angle. Steady boat.
Person: Take a firm grip on seat of chair and back of boat.

3

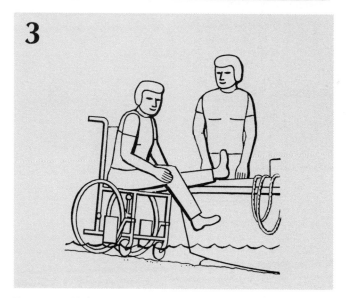

Person: Lift legs out of boat.

NOTE
It is best to reserve an old chair for this activity.

2

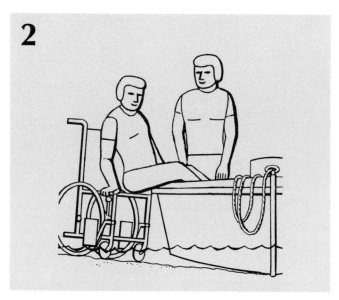

Person: Hitch buttocks up and over onto chair.

BOAT TO CHAIR ON WHARF

PARTLY ASSISTED
One helper required

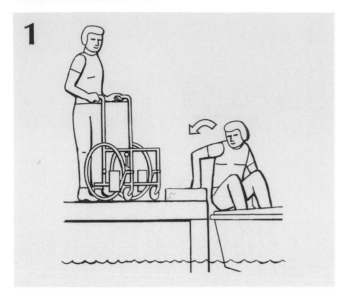

Helper: Securely moor boat in such a way as to prevent ropes hindering access. Position cushion on wharf. Steady chair.
Person: Press right hand on cushion and left hand on back of boat. Hitch buttocks up and over onto cushion.

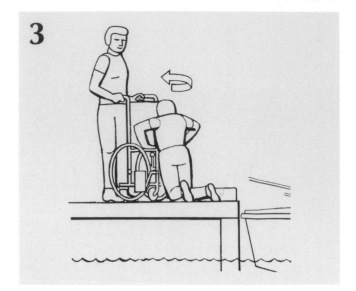

Person: Lean on seat of chair with hands and kneel in front of chair.
Helper: Make sure chair does not move.

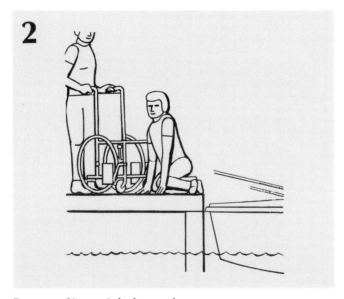

Person: Sit on right buttock.

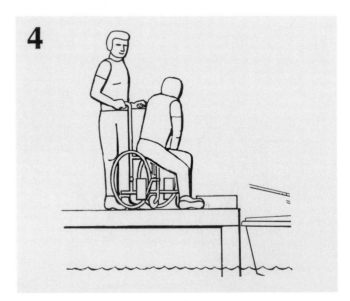

Person: Push down on hands to swing buttocks up and round into chair.

In chair movements

CORRECT SITTING POSITION

Correct sitting position is with hips and knees at right angles, and feet flat on the floor (or footplate). The upper body should be symmetrical in the chair, with weight evenly distributed to buttocks and thighs. The arms should be supported, if necessary, to maintain balance.

1

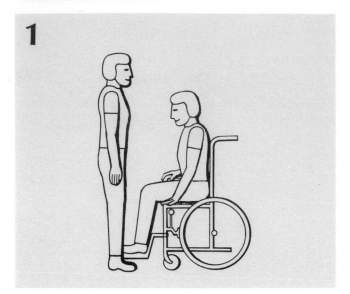

Make sure chair cannot slip. If person is in a wheelchair put brakes on.
Person: Put hands on arm-rests or seat of chair.

2

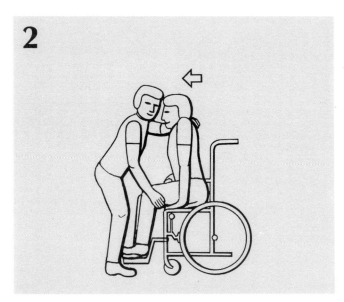

Person: Lean towards right and hitch left buttock forward in the seat.
Helper: Assist person to lean to right with your left hand on person's right shoulder. Assist person to hitch left buttock forward by lifting under person's left knee.

3

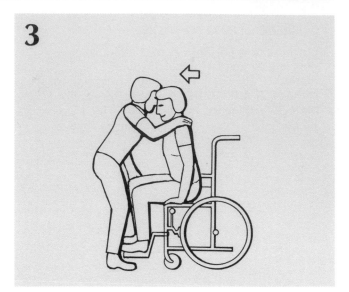

Person: Now lean towards left and hitch right buttock forward in the seat.
Helper: Assist person to lean to left with your right hand on person's left shoulder. Assist person to hitch right buttock forward by lifting under person's right knee. Repeat from side to side until person is in desired sitting position.

NOTE
This manoeuvre is useful in:
- *Correcting sitting position (see p. 123).*
- *Moving to front of seat prior to standing.*
- *Arranging clothing (e.g. in toiletting).*

Hip hitch

© Tony Pelosi and Margaret Gleeson 1988

1

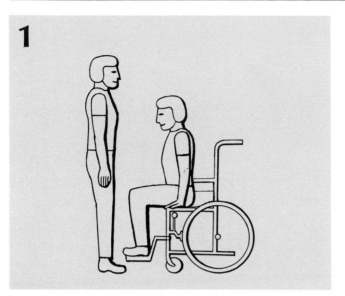

Make sure chair cannot slip. If person is in a wheelchair put brakes on.
Person: Put hands on arm-rests or seat of chair.

2

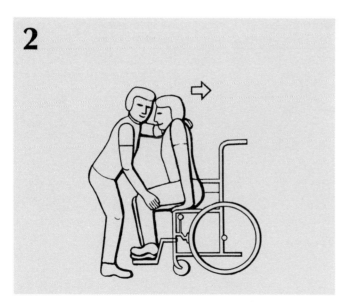

Person: Lean towards right and hitch left buttock back in the seat.
Helper: Assist person to lean to right with your left hand on person's right shoulder. Assist person to hitch left buttock back by lifting under left knee.

3

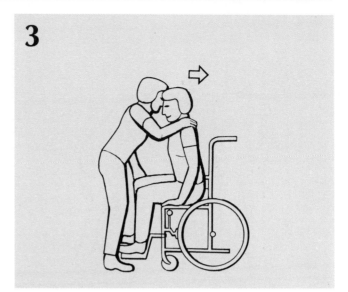

Person: Now lean towards left and hitch right buttock back in seat.
Helper: Assist person to lean to left with your right hand on person's left shoulder. Assist person to hitch right buttock back by lifting under right knee. Repeat from side to side until person is in desired sitting position.

NOTE
This manoeuvre is useful in:
* *Correcting sitting position (see p. 123).*
* *Moving to back of seat after sitting down.*

CORRECTING SITTING POSITION

MUCH ASSISTED
Two helpers required

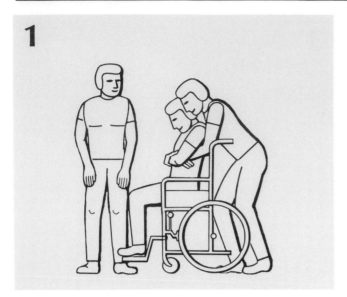

Make sure chair cannot slip. If person is in a wheelchair, put brakes on.
Helper 1: Stand behind the chair and take the person in a through-arm, wrist crossed-over grip. Lunge your forward knee into back of chair and bend other knee slightly.

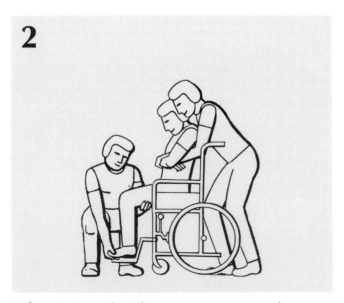

Helper 2: Squat beside person, one arm under person's thighs and other hand supporting person's feet.

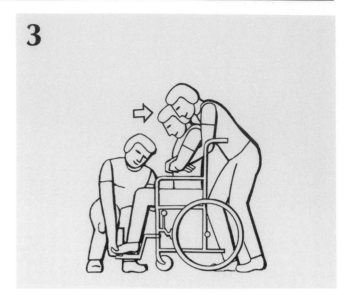

Helpers: On command '1–2–3–lift', move the person back or forward in the chair to the correct sitting position.

NOTE
The taller helper should be behind the chair.

Chair to floor transfers

11

The reverses of these manoeuvres (that is, getting up from the floor) are included in Chapter 12, Emergency transfers.

1

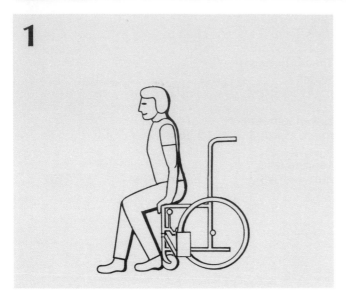

Park chair facing area. Brakes on, footplates swung away and arm-rests removed. Wriggle to front of seat and put both hands on seat. Put right foot forward and left foot back.

2

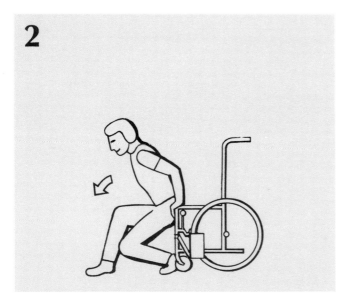

Push down on your hands and lower yourself onto your left knee. Bring right knee back and kneel on both knees.

3

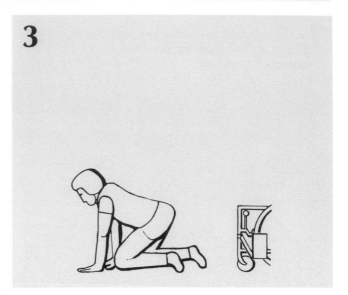

Put hands onto floor and crawl away from chair.

4

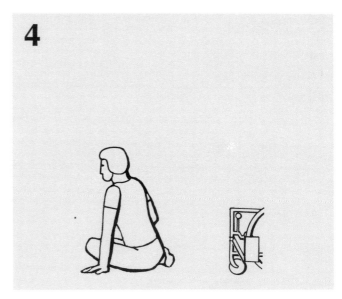

Sit down onto left buttock.

NOTE
Lower down onto the stronger leg, which is the left in this example.

1

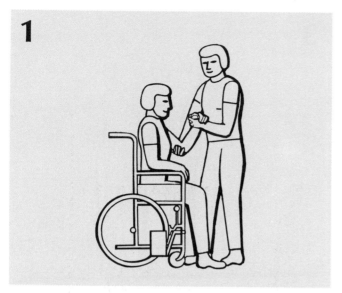

Park chair facing area. Brakes on and footplates swung away.
Helper: Take person's left hand in a thumb-through grip and hold person's elbow in your right hand.
Person: Put right hand on arm-rest. On command '1–2–3–stand'
Helper: Assist person to stand.
Person: Push on arm rest and pull on gripped hand to stand up.

2

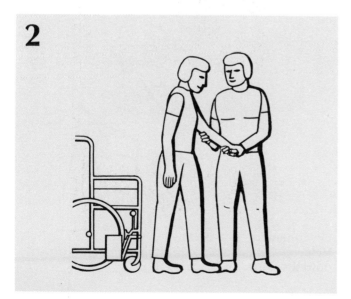

Person: Press down on helper's hand.
Helper: Support person on left side by allowing person to press down on left hand. Together walk forward away from chair.

3

When clear of chair, on command '1–2–3–bend'
Helper: Bend right knee onto floor, supporting person on the way down.
Person: Bend left knee onto floor with helper's support.

4

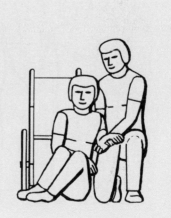

Person: Put right knee onto floor and sit down onto left buttock.
Helper: Maintain hand support with left hand and use right hand to guide person onto left buttock.

NOTE
Helper assists on stronger side, which is the left side in this example.

1

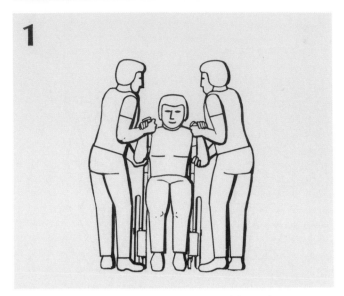

Park chair facing area. Brakes on and footplates swung away.
Helpers: Stand either side of person. Take person in a thumb-through grip with one hand, and support person's elbow with other hand.

2

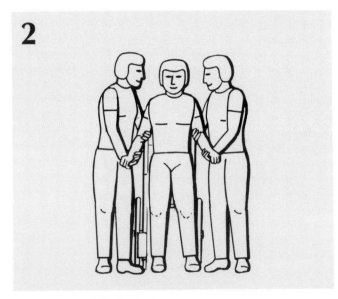

On command '1–2–3–stand'
Person: Pull on hand grips and stand up.
Helpers: Assist person to stand. Together walk forward for a few steps with person pushing down on helper's hands.

3

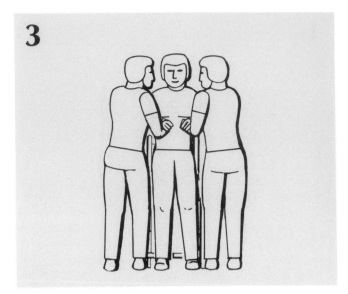

Helpers: About face, feet pointing toward chair, with near side foot back. Link inner arms with person and press against person's side. Support person's back with free arm.

4

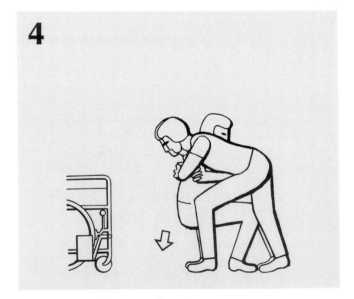

On command '1–2–3–down'
Helpers: Lunge forward to sit person gently down onto the floor.

NOTE
This manoeuvre is not suitable for a person with shoulder pain or frail shoulders.

1

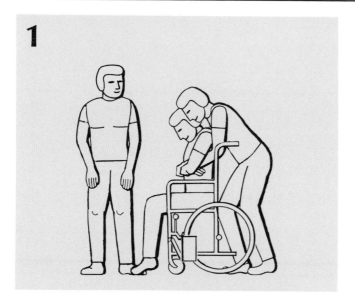

Park chair alongside area. Brakes on, footplates swung away and near side arm-rest removed.
Helper 1: Take person in a through-arm, wrist crossed-over grip. Lunge your forward knee into back of chair and bend other knee slightly.

2

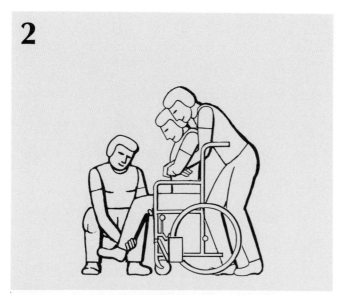

Helper 2: Squat beside person's legs, one arm under person's thighs and other under calves.

3

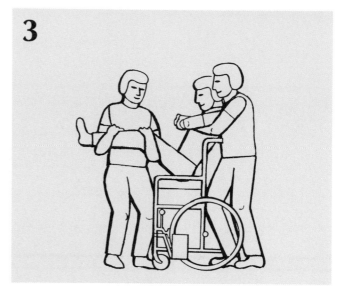

On command '1–2–3–lift'
Helpers: Straighten knees to lift person out of chair. Step clear of chair.

4

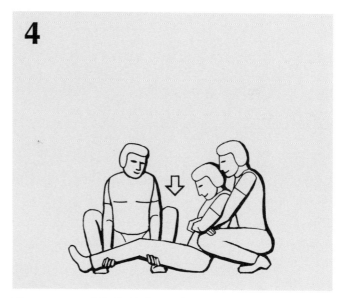

On command '1–2–3–lower'
Helpers: Squat down to lower person onto the floor.

NOTE
1. *The taller helper should be behind the chair.*
2. *This lift is not suitable with a heavy person; use a hoist if available.*

Emergency transfers

12

There may be occasions when the person who has had a fall is unconscious. Attempts to move the person should be delayed until professional help is available. However, basic first-aid rules apply:

1. Make sure the airways are clear (remove false teeth, food particles etc.)
2. Place person in the coma position (Fig. 12.1).
3. Apply any other first aid necessary, and get help.

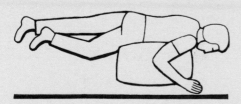

Fig. 12.1 Coma position

1

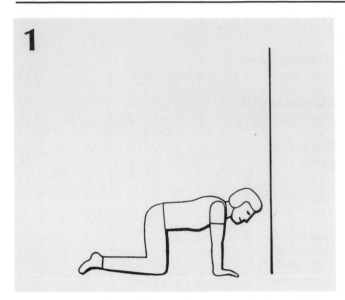

Turn onto hands and knees facing a wall. If possible, next to a door-frame or other support.

3

Stand while walking hands up wall and bring right leg forward.

NOTE
Always lead with strong leg first, which is the left leg in this example.

2

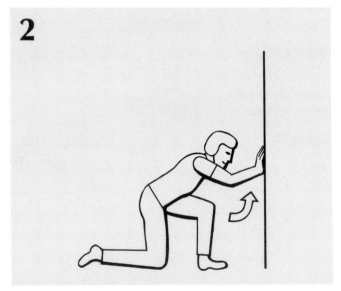

Put left leg up so foot is flat on floor. Place hands on wall and/or door-frame and lean into wall.

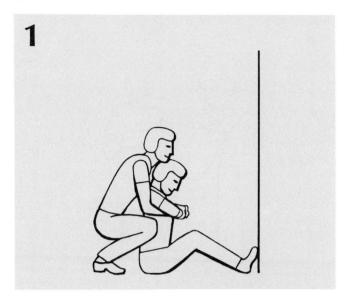

Helper: After checking that there is no serious injury, roll person onto back. Squat behind person and take a through-arm, wrist crossed-over grip. Make sure person's feet are blocked to prevent slipping, and assist person into sitting. Squat again.

Helper: Assist person into standing by straightening your knees.

NOTE
This manoeuvre is impractical when the person is very heavy and/or tall and the helper is small. Seek assistance from another helper.

FALL IN CONFINED SPACE

MUCH ASSISTED
Two helpers required

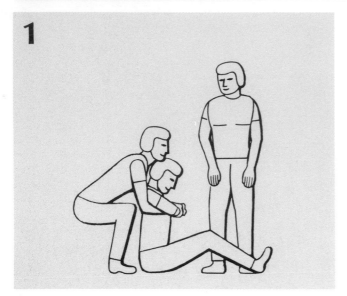

Helpers: After checking that there is no serious injury roll person onto back.
Helper 1: Squat behind person and raise their shoulders slightly to take a through-arm, wrist crossed-over grip. Assist into sitting position by straightening knees. Squat again.

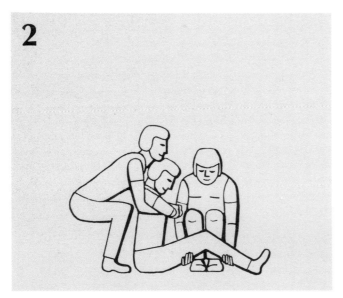

Helper 2: Squat at person's knees and put one arm under the thighs and one under the calves.

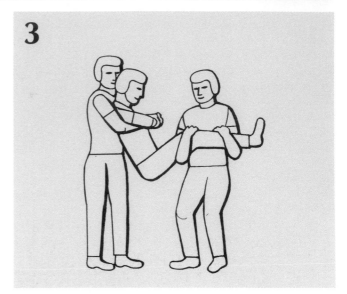

Helpers: On command '1–2–3–lift', stand up and carry person to chair or bed.

NOTE
1. *Make sure there is enough room for three people before carrying out this manoeuvre.*
2. *The taller helper should be at the person's head.*

Half kneel pivot (high and low supports)

1

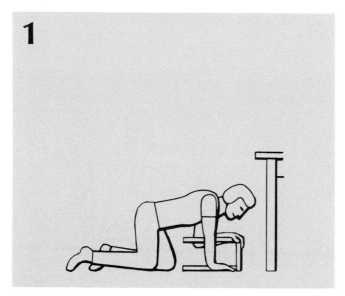

Turn onto hands and knees and crawl to stable support (e.g. sink, table). Take with you low support (e.g. stool).

2

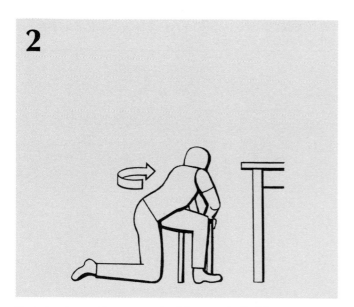

Put stool next to support with your left side alongside stool. Bring left foot forward with foot on floor. Place hands over onto stool.

3

Push down on hands and foot and swivel buttocks onto stool.

4

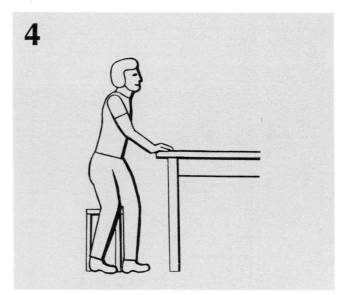

Place hands onto higher support. Push/pull on hands and feet, and stand up.

NOTE
Movement should be led by the stronger side, which is the left side in this example.

1

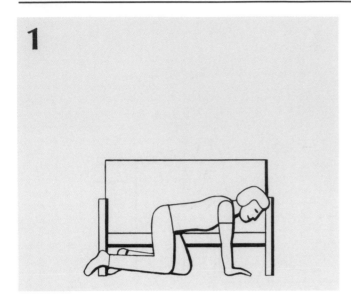

Turn onto hands and knees and crawl to stable support (e.g. couch, chair) with left side alongside support.

2

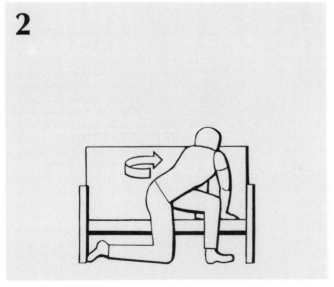

Bring left foot forward with foot on floor. Place hands on support.

3

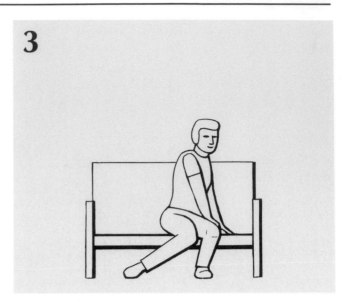

Push down on hands and foot, lift and swivel your buttocks up onto support.

NOTE
Movement should be led by the stronger side, which is the left side in this example.

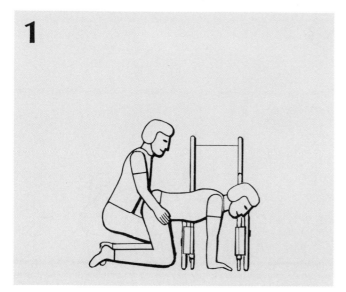

1

Helper: After first checking that there is no serious injury, park wheelchair beside person. Put brakes on, swing foot plates away and remove near side arm-rest.
Helper: Squat down and assist person onto hands and knees, with left side next to chair.

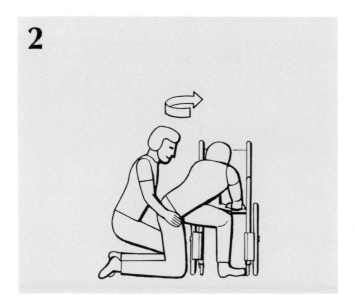

2

Person: Put hands on seat. Bend left leg to put foot on floor.

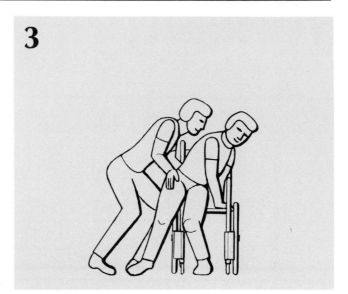

3

On command '1–2–3–push'
Person: Push down on hands to lift and swivel buttocks into chair.
Helper: Support and lift at person's hips.

NOTE
1. *Movement should be led by the stronger side, which is the left side in this example.*
2. *If chair seat is too high, move first onto a low stool and then into the chair.*

MUCH ASSISTED
Two helpers required

1

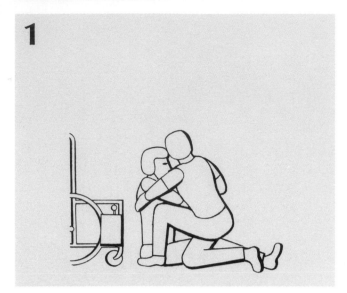

Helper: After checking that there is no serious injury, park wheelchair behind person. Brakes on, footplates swung away and arm-rests removed.
Helpers: Half kneel on either side of the person, facing the wheelchair. Assist the person into sitting using thumb-through grip and shoulder-blade grip.

2

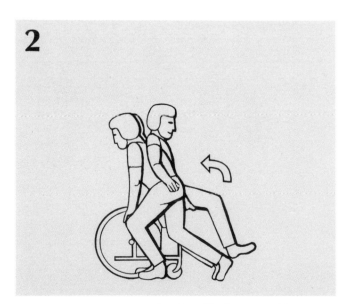

Person: Rest arms over backs of helpers and lean forward.
Helpers: Press near side shoulder into person's armpit and put this hand beneath thighs of person to clasp wrist of other helper. Put other hand on your knee and push hand down on your knee as you straighten your legs. Make sure your head is between person and wheelchair.

3

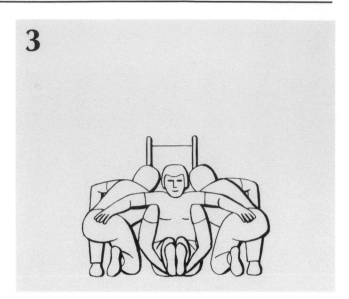

Helpers: On command '1–2–3–lift', press into the person's chest firmly and lift person up and back into chair.

NOTE
This is not suitable with a heavy person. Use a mechanical hoist.

FALL IN OPEN SPACE
MUCH ASSISTED
Two helpers required

1

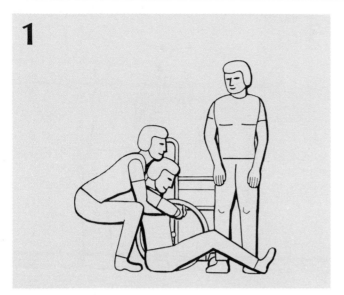

Helper 1: After checking that there is no serious injury, park wheelchair beside person. Brakes on, footplates swung away and near side arm-rest removed. Squat down at head of person and take a through-arm, wrist crossed-over grip. Assist person into sitting by straightening your knees. Squat again.

2

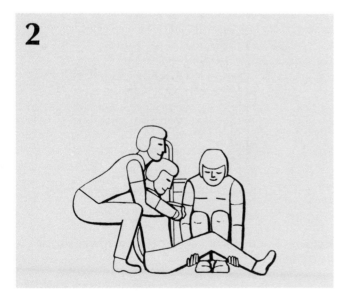

Helper 2: Squat beside person, one arm under person's thighs and other under calves.

3

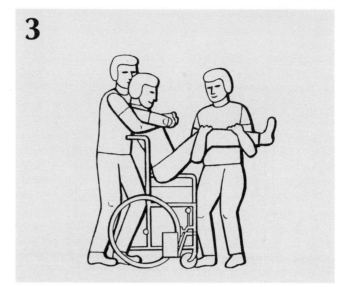

Helpers: On command '1–2–3–lift', straighten legs to lift the person up and walk to wheelchair. Lower person into chair.

NOTE
1. *The taller helper should be at the head of the person.*
2. *This lift is not suitable with a heavy person. Use a mechanical hoist.*

MUCH ASSISTED
One helper required

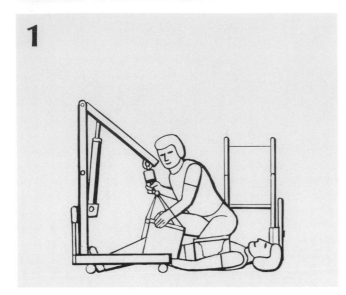

1

Helper: After first checking that there is no serious injury, park wheelchair beside person. Brakes on, footplates swung away and arm-rests removed. Position sling under person. Position hoist close to person and wheelchair. Put brakes on hoist.

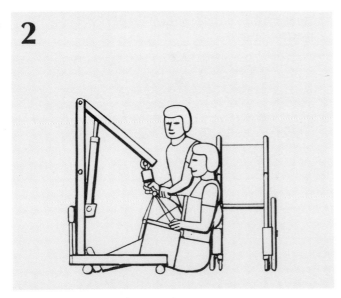

2

Helper: Connect slings to hoist.

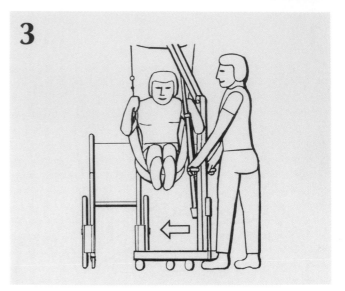

3

Helper: Lift person and rotate hoist to position person over wheelchair. Move chair if necessary.

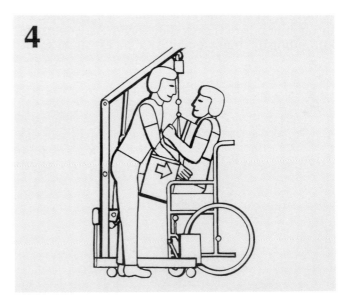

4

Helper: Stand in front of person and lower slowly into chair.

Cradle lift

© Tony Pelosi and Margaret Gleeson 1988

Helpers: After first checking that there is no serious injury, squat to face each other at either side of person. Assist person into sitting. Take a wrist grip under person's thighs and behind person's back.

NOTE
This lift is not recommended. It has been demonstrated to produce extreme spinal strain in the helpers and should be used only when no other options are available. Do not use this lift with heavy people.

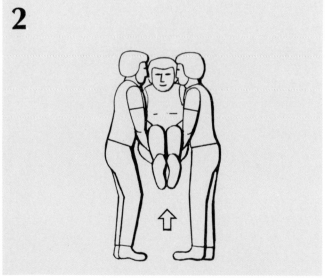

Helpers: Make sure one foot is pointing towards person and other foot is pointing in direction of planned movement. On command '1–2–3–lift', brace and straighten knees to lift person, and carry to chair or bed.

Management of spasticity

INTRODUCTION

Spasticity (or spasm) is a complicated physiological phenomenon which occurs in association with some neurological disorders. This chapter offers a brief explanation of spasticity and some practical techniques to assist people whose spasticity hinders their everyday activities.

In simple terms, spasticity is the development of an unusual increase in tone in a muscle or group of muscles. The muscles at rest do not have excessive tone but develop an unusual increase in tone when the body part is moved or placed in certain postures. Similarly, the muscles may develop this increased tone in response to other stimuli, such as when the person is surprised or touched unexpectedly, when the person makes a strong effort to do an activity, or when the person sneezes or coughs.

When this unusual increase in muscle tone (spasticity) is present, the body part feels stiff and is difficult for the person or the helper to move. In this way spasticity often interferes with free voluntary movement and reduces the person's independence. The correct management of spasticity can assist the person with a disability and the helper to minimize the degree to which spasticity predominates and/or to cope in situations where it has become a problem.

Spasticity can be present in many complex combinations of muscle groups and its presence will vary from individual to individual and from time to time. However, it is mostly exhibited in two basic patterns: flexor spasticity and extensor spasticity. For practical purposes we will only consider the management of these two patterns of spasticity.

Flexor spasticity

The general tendency of flexor spasticity is for a pattern of 'limb bending' to develop. In the arm, this is characterized by the arm wanting to cross over the body, with the elbow bent, and with the wrist and fingers curled.

In the leg, it is exhibited by the hip, knee, ankle and big toe being bent upward and the other toes splayed apart.

Extensor spasticity

The general tendency of extensor spasticity is for a pattern of 'limb straightening' to develop. Extensor spasticity in the arm can be considered rare and is thus not discussed.

In the leg, extensor spasticity is exhibited by the leg tending to cross over the other leg, with the knee straight, the foot pressed down and inward, and the toes curled under.

Ankle clonus

Quite often, a person with a neurological disorder will also demonstrate an involuntary tapping of the foot which may interfere with their activities. The term for this repetitive tapping is ankle clonus. Clonus is also due to the state of unusual increase in muscle tone and is set off at the ankle by a stretch of the calf muscles.

MANAGEMENT OF SPASTICITY

The basic principle of the management of spasticity is to maintain the body part in a position opposite to the usual pattern of spasticity. That is to say, if the arm is usually curled up across the body it should be positioned as straight as possible away from the body. This discourages the development of spasticity. In addition, it is important when assisting a person with spasticity to handle them slowly and gently, since jerky movements usually increase the spasticity. When changing the position of a limb, time should be given for the limb to adjust to the movement and to the new position. Similarly, a person transferring should be allowed time to lie, sit or stand in the new position before moving on to the next step in the transfer.

Once present, the spasticity can be so severe that it may cause the person to slip out of the chair. Care should be taken to minimize such risks by adequately positioning and/or restraining the limb(s) in the chair. In bed, extra pillows increase safety and allow effective positioning of the person, and reduce the likelihood of spasticity predominating.

Some specific techniques of management of spasticity are shown on the following pages. Since many of these techniques require the use of extra pillows under the bedding, oversized blankets (for example, a double-bed size on a single bed) are recommended.

Positioning to minimize extensor spasticity in legs

1

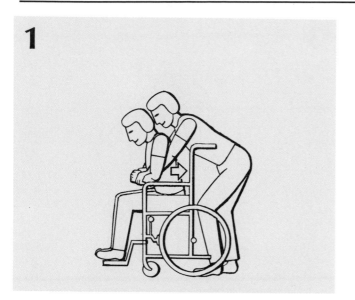

Helper: Make sure chair can't slip. If person is in wheelchair, put brakes on. Make sure person's buttocks are as far back in chair as possible (see p. 125).

2

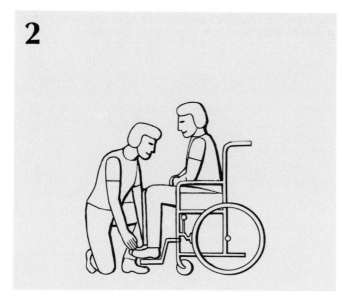

Helper: Make sure whole of person's foot is in contact with floor or footplates.

3

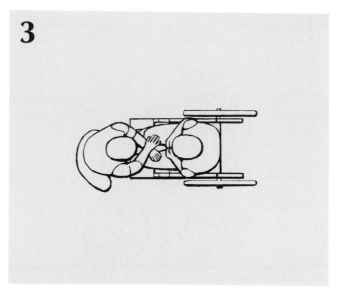

Helper: Separate person's knees with firm steady outward pressure from your hands.

4

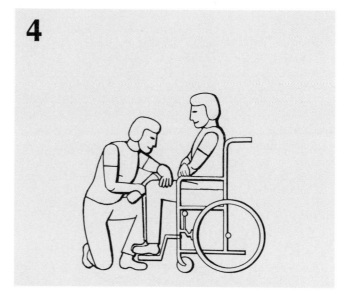

Helper: Place a small block of firm rubber or a folded towel between knees to maintain separation.

NOTE
1. *To prevent increasing spasticity during the manoeuvre, avoid pressure on balls of feet. Avoid jerky movements.*
2. *In severe cases a shin strap or toe loops can be fitted to chair (see Ch. 3).*
3. *The wheelchair can be modified to make the seat higher at the front than at the back, to discourage extensor spasm.*

IN A CHAIR
PARTLY ASSISTED
One helper

1

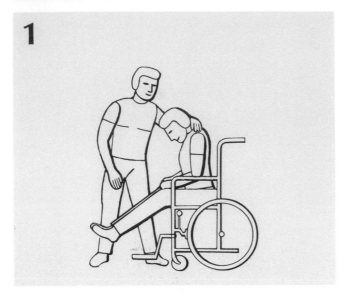

Helper: Make sure chair can't slip. If person is in wheelchair put brakes on. Tell person to tuck chin onto chest and to lean forward if possible.

2

Helper: Crouch beside person's knee. Put one arm under knees and hold toes with other hand. Apply firm steady pressure with both hands and bend person's knees and feet back. Wait until spasm subsides, then slowly remove hands.

3

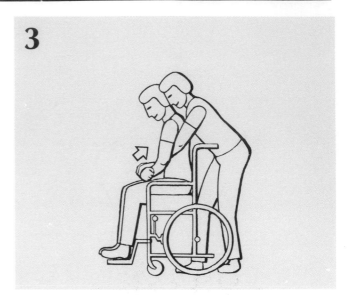

Helper: Take a through-arm, wrist crossed-over grip. Lunge knee into back of chair and assist person into correct sitting position (see p. 123).

NOTE
To prevent increasing spasticity during manoeuvre, avoid pressure on balls of feet. Avoid jerky movements.

Relieving moderate extensor spasticity in legs

1

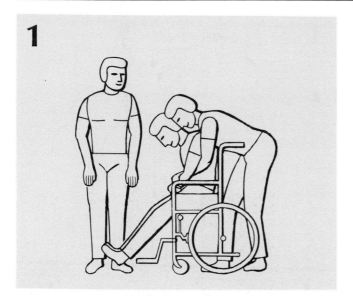

Helper 1: Make sure chair can't slip. If person is in wheelchair put brakes on. Take through-arm, wrist crossed-over grip. Lunge knee into back of chair. Assist person to bend forward and hold position

2

Helper 2: Crouch beside person's knees. Put one arm under knees and hold toes with other hand. Apply firm, steady pressure with both hands and bend person's knees and feet back.

3

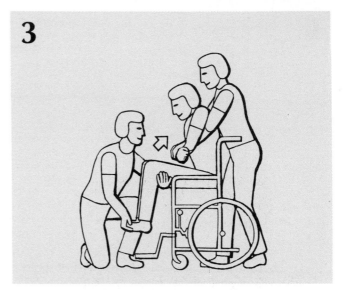

Helpers: Wait till spasm subsides. On command '1–2–3–lift', move person back in chair to correct sitting position (see p. 123).

NOTE
To prevent increasing spasticity during the manoeuvre, avoid pressure on the balls of feet. Avoid jerky movements.

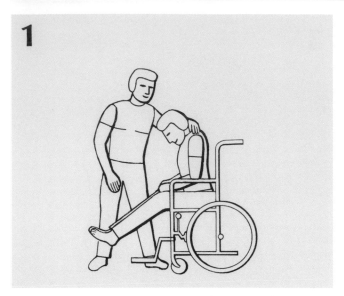

Helper: Make sure chair can't slip. If person is in wheelchair put brakes on. Tell person to tuck chin onto chest and to lean forward if possible.

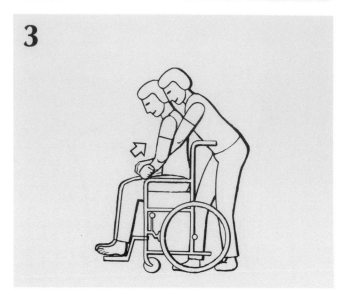

Helper: Take a through-arm, wrist crossed-over grip. Lunge knee into back of chair and assist person into correct sitting position (see p. 123).

NOTE
To prevent increasing spasm during manoeuvre, avoid pressure on the balls of the feet. Avoid jerky movements.

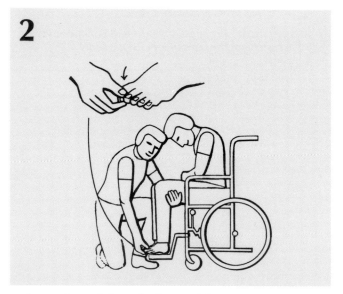

Helper: Crouch beside person's knees. Put one arm under knees and bend big toe of near leg down. Bend big toe of far leg down. Person's legs will bend in a reflex action. Hold feet and knees in a bent position until spasm subsides.

© Tony Pelosi and Margaret Gleeson 1988

1

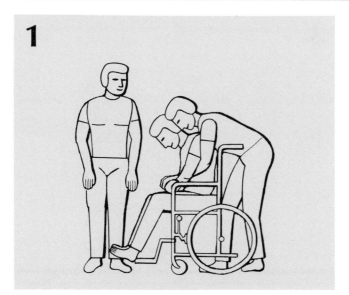

Helper 1: Make sure chair can't slip. If person is in wheelchair, put brakes on. Take through-arm, wrist crossed-over grip. Lunge knee into back of chair. Assist person to bend forward and hold position.

2

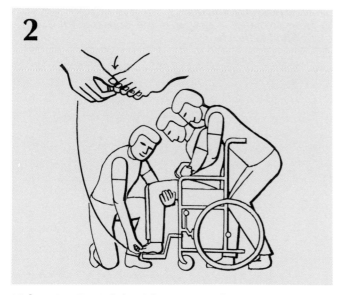

Helper 2: Crouch beside person's knees. Put one arm under knees and bend big toe of near leg down. Bend big toe of far leg down. Person's legs will bend in a reflex action. Hold feet and knees in a bent position until spasm subsides.

3

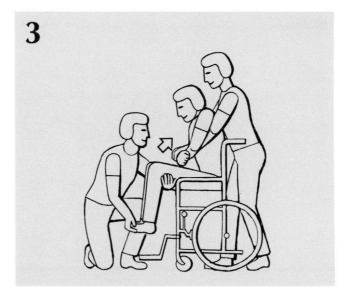

Helpers: On command '1–2–3–lift', move person back in chair to correct sitting position (see p. 123).

NOTE
To prevent increasing spasticity during manoeuvre avoid pressure on balls of feet. Avoid jerky movements.

1

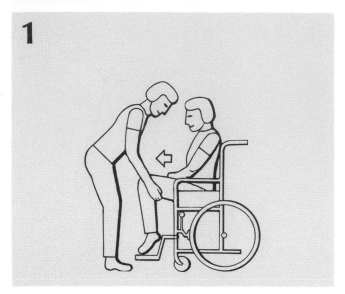

Helper: Make sure chair can't slip. If person is in wheelchair, put brakes on. Make sure person's buttocks are slightly away from back of seat.

2

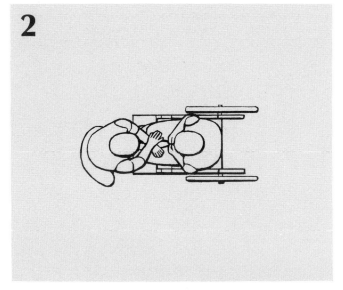

Helper: Cross arms and place hands on inside of person's knees. Separate knees with firm steady downward and outward pressure from your hands.

3

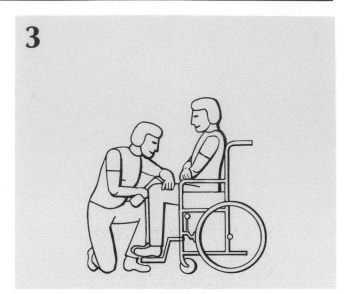

Helper: Place small block of firm rubber or folded towel between knees to maintain separation.

NOTE
1. *To prevent increasing spasticity during the manoeuvre, avoid jerky movements.*
2. *In severe cases, a leg strap or toe loops (see Ch. 3) can be fitted to the chair.*

Relieving flexor spasticity in legs

1

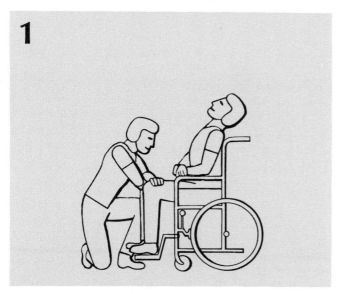

Helper: Make sure chair can't slip. If person is in wheelchair put brakes on. Tell person to push head back as far as possible.

2

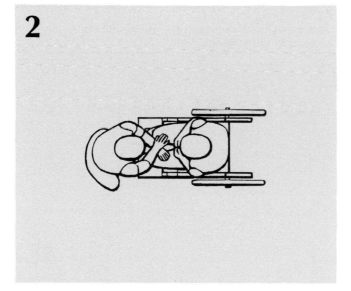

Helper: Cross arms and place hands on inside of person's knees. Separate knees with firm, steady downward and outward pressure from your hands.

3

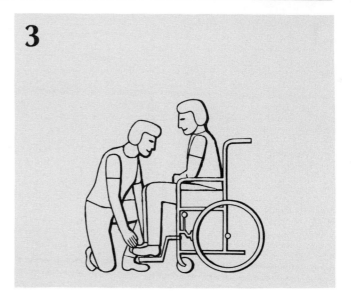

Helper: When spasm subsides, position feet on floor or footplates. Place small block of firm rubber or folded towel between knees to maintain separation.

NOTE
To prevent increasing spasticity during the manoeuvre, avoid jerky movements.

1

2

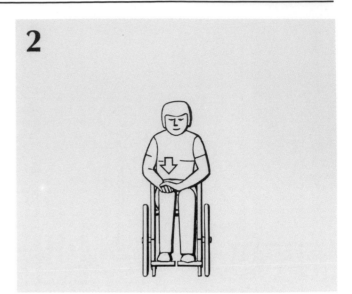

If in wheelchair put brakes on. Lift thigh and reposition foot on footplate (or floor) so that heel will come into contact with footplate when knee is pressed down.

Put hand(s) on top of knee, lean forward and push down through leg. Hold steady pressure until tapping subsides. Repeat if tapping recurs.

NOTE
To prevent increasing spasticity during the manoeuvre, avoid jerky movements.

Relieving ankle clonus (heel tapping)

1

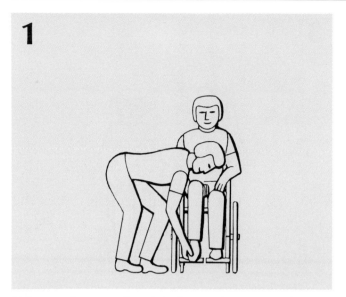

Helper: Place one hand underneath person's thigh and hold toes with other hand. Slowly reposition foot so that heel will come in contact with footplate when knee is pressed down.

2

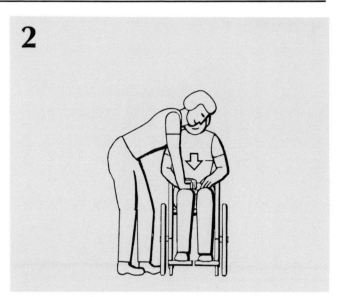

Helper: Place hand on person's knee and apply strong pressure down through leg. Hold pressure until tapping subsides. Repeat if tapping recurs.

NOTE
To prevent increasing spasticity during the manoeuvre, avoid jerky movements.

1

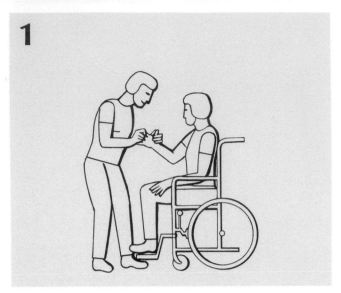

Helper: Tell person to turn head toward arm with spasticity. Slowly but firmly open fingers and spread thumb away from palm. As spasticity subsides, bend wrist back and maintain hand open whilst straightening elbow.

2

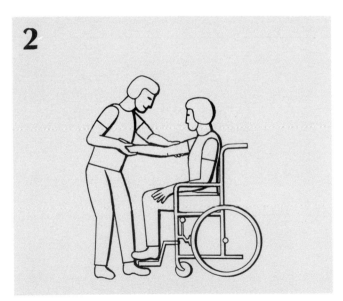

Helper: Take person's arm away from body and hold extended until you are able to position it correctly, that is, when the elbow will stay in a half-bent position without further bending.

3

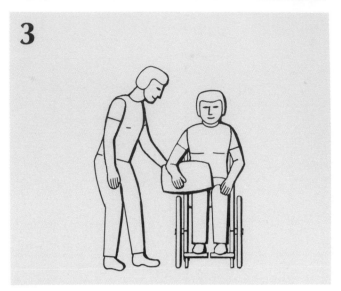

Helper: Position arm on arm-rest of chair or pillow, so that arm remains away from body with elbow half-bent and fingers and wrist supported in a flat position.

NOTE
1. *To prevent increasing spasticity during the manoeuvre, avoid jerky movements.*
2. *A short, hard cylinder (5 cm diameter) placed in the hand will minimize flexor spasticity.*
3. *Use a chair with arms, as flexor spasticity in the arm can cause a person to topple sideways and forwards out of the chair.*

Positioning to minimize extensor spasticity in legs

© Tony Pelosi and Margaret Gleeson 1988

ON SIDE

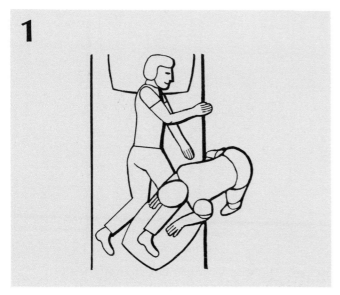

Helper: Place pillow under top leg with knees bent.

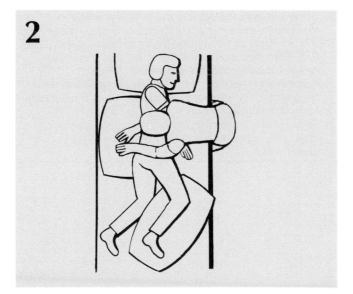

Helper: Place pillow behind back to prevent the person rolling back.

ON BACK

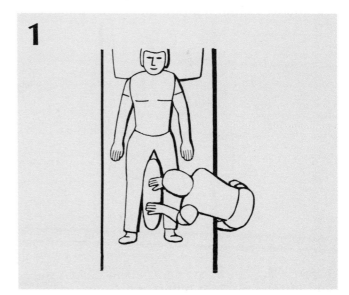

Helper: Separate person's legs and place a pillow between knees.

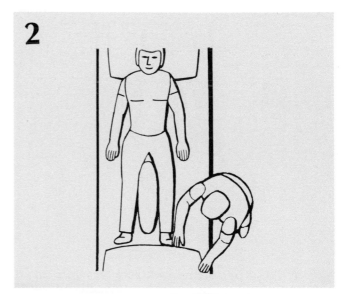

Helper: Put pillow at feet to lift weight of bedclothes.

NOTE
1. *To prevent increasing spasticity during the manoeuvre, avoid pressure on the balls of the feet. Avoid jerky movements.*
2. *Do not put pillow behind person's knees as this may hinder circulation.*
3. *Alternating these positions will help prevent pressure areas.*

1

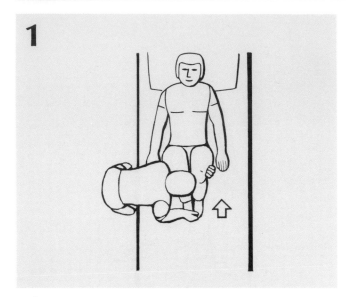

Helper: Place one hand under person's thighs and hold person's toes with other hand. Gently and firmly bend both legs up and put feet flat on bed.

2

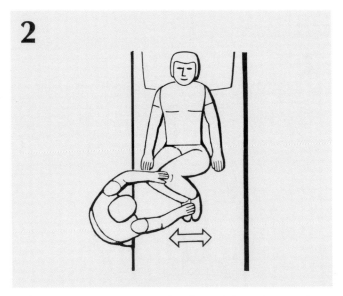

Helper: Assist person to slowly rock legs from side until spasticity subsides.

3

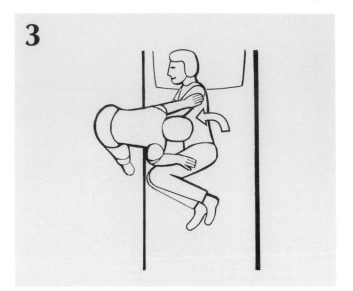

Helper: Without letting knees straighten, assist person to turn onto side with bent knees. Position person to minimize spasticity (see p. 157).

NOTE
1. *This is also useful preparation for a person wishing to sit up and over the edge of the bed, especially first thing in the morning when spasticity is often more severe. (Very often, a person with extensor spasm will find that when he moves in bed, his legs shoot out straight, making further movement difficult.)*
2. *If spasticity is very strong, a firm bending down of the big toe may elicit reflex bending and allow the leg to be bent at the hip and knee.*
3. *To prevent increasing spasticity during manoeuvre, avoid pressure on balls of the feet. Avoid jerky movements.*

Positioning to minimize flexor spasticity in legs

ON SIDE

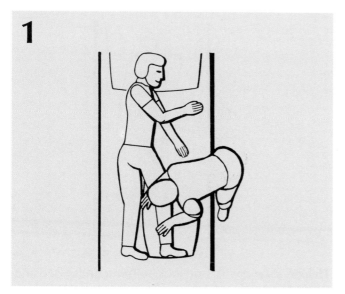

Helper: Place pillow under top leg with both legs as straight as possible.

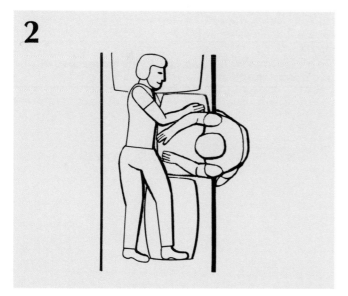

Helper: Place pillow in front of person to prevent person rolling forward.

Helper: Place pillow at feet to lift weight of bedclothes.

ON BACK

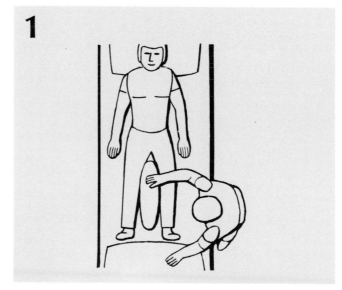

Helper: Separate person's legs and place pillow between knees. Position person's legs as straight as possible in bed. Place pillow at feet to lift weight of bedclothes.

NOTE
1. *To prevent increasing spasticity during the manoeuvre, avoid jerky movements.*
2. *Do not put pillow behind person's knees, as this may hinder circulation.*
3. *Alternating these positions will help prevent pressure areas.*

PARTLY ASSISTED
One helper

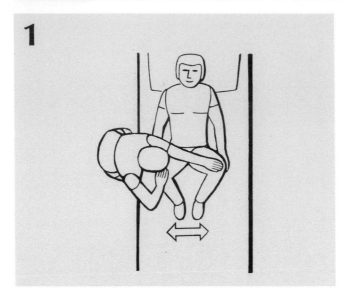

1

Helper: Place hands on inside of person's knees. Press knees apart gently and firmly whilst slowly rocking person's legs from side to side. As spasm subsides slowly decrease hand pressure.

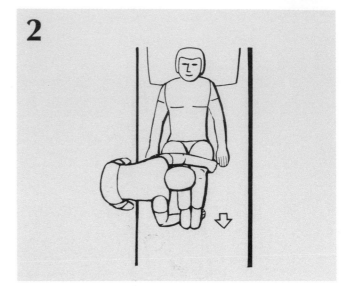

2

Helper: Stand with one foot pointing under bed and other in line of movement. Put one arm across thighs and other arm under heels. Progressively straighten legs. Hold pressure until spasm subsides and then slowly remove hands. Position person to minimize spasticity (see p. 157).

NOTE
To prevent increasing spasticity during the manoeuvre, avoid jerky movements.

Positioning to minimize flexor spasticity in arm

© Tony Pelosi and Margaret Gleeson 1988

ON SIDE

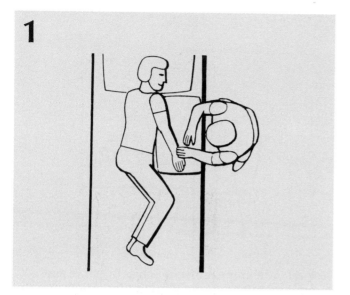

1

Helper: Place pillow under top arm with elbow as straight as possible and shoulder forward.

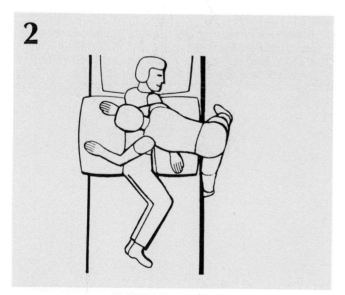

2

Helper: Place another pillow behind back. Underneath arm can lie straight alongside body or bent beneath pillow, whichever position is the more comfortable.

ON BACK

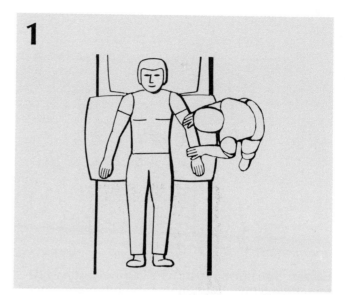

1

Helper: Place pillow on each side of person. Rest arms on pillows with elbows as straight as possible. Wrist and hands supported flat on pillow.

NOTE
1. *To prevent increasing spasticity during the manoeuvre, avoid jerky movements.*
2. *Alternating these positions will help prevent pressure areas.*
3. *A short, hard cylinder (5 cm diameter) placed in the hand will help minimize flexor spasticity.*

1

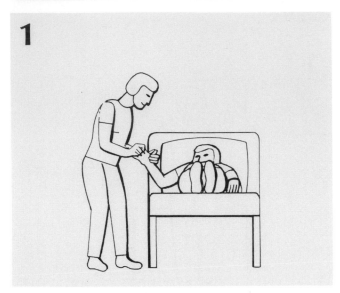

Helper: Tell person to turn head toward arm with spasticity. Slowly but firmly open fingers and spread thumb away from palm.

2

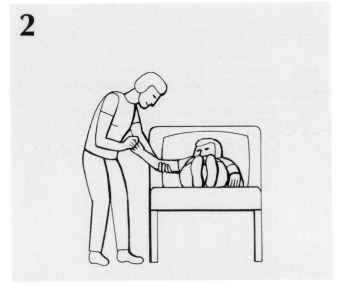

Helper: As spasticity subsides, bend wrist back and maintain hand open whilst straightening elbow. Keep person's fingers straight and wrist bent back with one hand, and hold arm just above elbow with other hand.

3

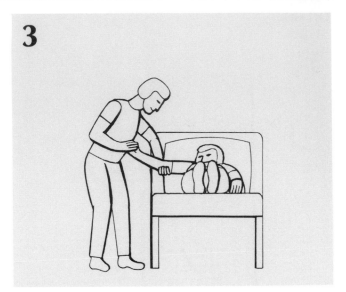

Helper: Straighten arm as much as possible and move it away from body. Hold until spasticity has subsided and arm can be positioned correctly. Position person to minimize spasticity (see p. 161).

NOTE
1. *To prevent increasing spasticity during the manoeuvre avoid jerky movements.*
2. *A short, hard cylinder (5 cm diameter) placed in the hand will help minimize flexor spasticity.*

TIPPING LEVER

All rear wheel drive chairs have tipping levers to enable the small front wheels to be tipped up when a vertical obstacle (e.g. kerb) is encountered. The chair is tipped by the helper putting his foot on the lever and leaning his weight through the foot and the two handles of the chair. Use of the tipping lever makes assisting a wheelchair user a much easier task.

HAZARDOUS TECHNIQUES

Some techniques shown here are hazardous without proper training and supervised practice, e.g. forwards down a kerb unassisted. It is strongly recommended that the helper familiarizes himself with the chair and the abilities of the user.

MAINTENANCE

General commonsense maintenance on wheelchairs prolongs their useful life and makes their use easier for those who need them.

Properly inflated pneumatic tyres will make it easier for helper and wheelchair user to push the chair — particularly over soft ground.

The brakes should be easy for the user to apply, but be firm enough to stop the wheel turning on a moderate grade (1 in 6).

Reference to the manual supplied with most chairs will provide adequate advice.

MUCH ASSISTED
One helper required

1

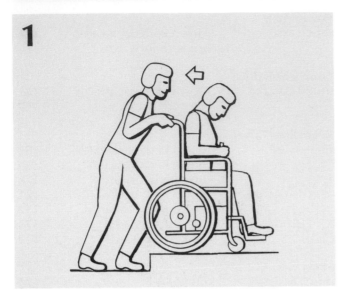

Helper: Help person line up back wheels square with kerb.
Person: Drive slowly backwards keeping head bent forward.

2

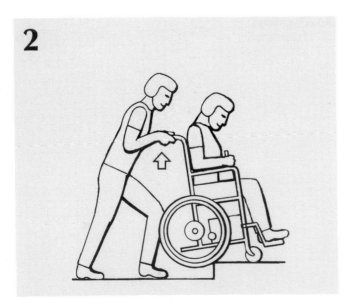

Helper: Lower chair slowly into gutter by lifting upwards on handles. Prevent bumping.

3

Helper: Tilt chair backwards by using tipping lever.
Person: Drive slowly backwards till footplates are clear of kerb.

4

Helper: Slowly lower front wheels.

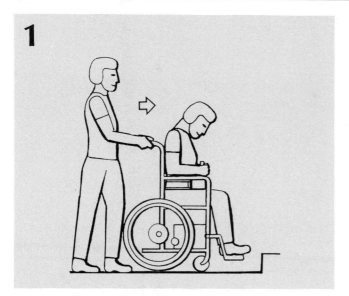

1

Person: Approach kerb squarely, bend head forward.

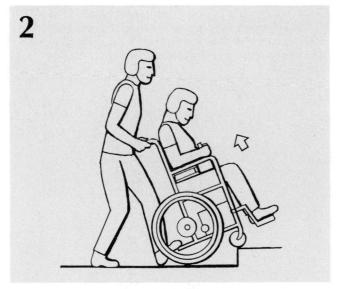

2

Helper: Tilt chair backwards by using tipping lever, and place front wheels onto kerb.
Person: Drive forward slowly.

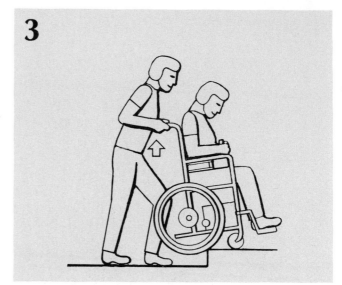

3

Person: Drive forward slowly.
Helper: Bend knees and grip handles. Lift on handles by straightening knees until rear wheels are on kerb.

NOTE
With some heavy chairs a second helper may be needed. If so, each take one side of the chair.

MUCH ASSISTED
One helper required

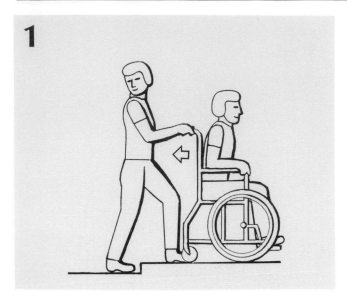

1

Helper: Approach kerb backwards and step down with one foot. Other foot up on kerb. Both pointing towards chair.
Person: Keep head bent forward.

3

Helper: Pull chair backwards, controlling descent of front wheels with downward pressure on handles.

NOTE
Because the footplates are generally lower on these chairs, they will probably scrape on the kerb in this manoeuvre. With high kerbs this manoeuvre may be impossible.

2

Helper: Keep small wheels in contact with kerb to prevent swivelling. Allow small wheels to roll down kerb slowly.

FRONT WHEEL DRIVE
MUCH ASSISTED
One helper required

1

Helper: Make sure the person is secured into wheelchair with a belt. Approach kerb backwards.

2

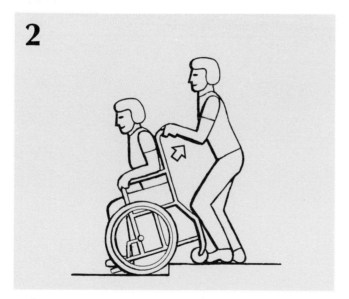

Helper: Stand up on kerb. Bend knees and lift handles to raise small wheels clear of kerb. Step backwards and roll small wheels backwards.

3

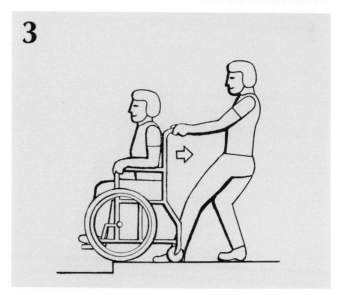

Helper: Lean down on wheelchair handles, lunge back, and at the same time pull chair so that large front wheels also come up onto kerb.

NOTE
1. *Care must be taken not to tip the person out of the chair when tilting.*
2. *Because the footplates are generally lower on these chairs, they will probably scrape on the ground in this manoeuvre. With high kerbs this manoeuvre may be impossible.*

UNASSISTED

© Tony Pelosi and Margaret Gleeson 1988

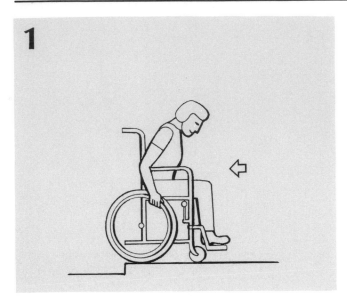

1

Back up to kerb until large rear wheels are square to kerb.

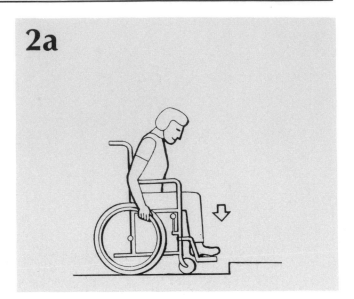

2a

NOTE
1. *Keep head bent forward throughout the manoeuvre.*
2. *Check the height of the kerb. If too great the footplates will catch on the kerb, in which case the forward descent or a helper is required.*

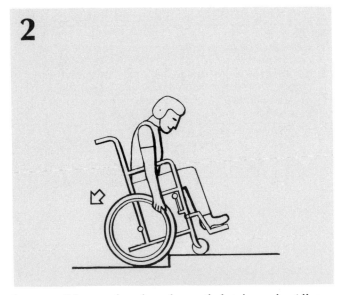

2

Lean well forward and push gently backwards. Allow large rear wheels and then small wheels to roll down kerb, and control descent of chair by pushing forwards on hand rims.

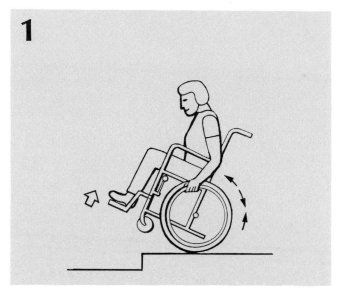

1

At kerb tilt chair back onto large rear wheels by leaning head forward, pulling back and giving a sharp extra push forward on hand rims of wheels.

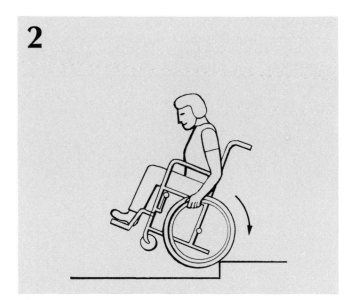

2

Keep chair tilted and balanced and move it slowly forwards over edge of kerb. Control descent by pulling back on hand rims until large wheels touch ground.

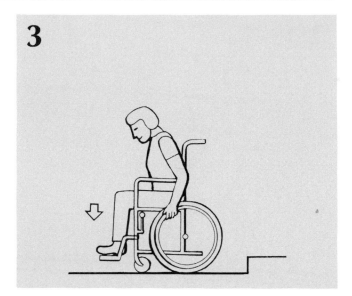

3

Lower small wheels onto ground.

NOTE
1. *Keep head bent forward throughout manoeuvre.*
2. *It is important that both large rear wheels contact the ground at the same time.*
3. *This manoeuvre requires a great deal of supervised practice.*

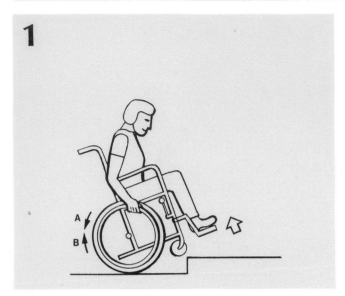

1

Approach kerb squarely. Do not touch kerb. Tilt chair back onto large rear wheels by leaning head forward, pulling wheels back (A) and giving a sharp extra push forward (B) on the hand rims.

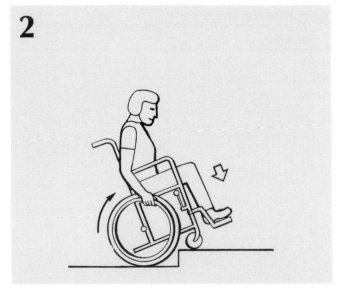

2

Keeping chair tilted and balanced, move castors over kerb. Lower castors down onto kerb.

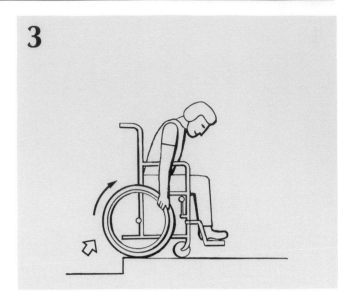

3

Lean forward again and with another sharp push forward on hand rims bring large rear wheels up onto kerb.

NOTE
1. *Keep head bent forward throughout the manoeuvre.*
2. *This manoeuvre requires a great deal of supervised practice.*

1

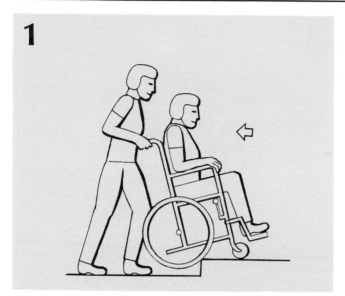

Helper: Back wheelchair squarely up to kerb. Lift up on handles taking some weight off large rear wheels. Step down kerb allowing large rear wheels to roll slowly down kerb.
Person: Bend head forward.

2

Helper: When rear wheels are in gutter, push foot down on tipping lever and hands down on handles and tilt wheelchair backwards onto large rear wheels. Hold chair tilted and balanced backwards and pull chair away from kerb.

3

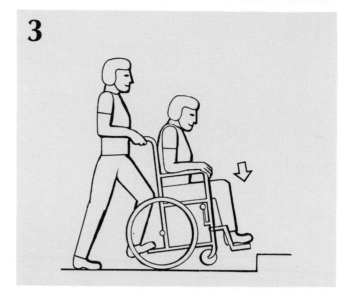

Helper: Put weight on tipping lever and gently lower small front wheels onto ground.

NOTE
Person must keep head bent forward throughout manoeuvre.

MUCH ASSISTED
One helper required

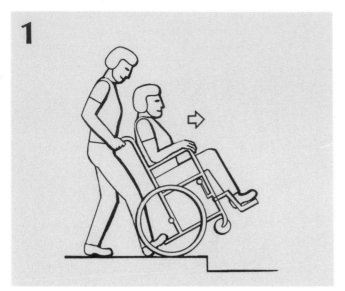

Helper: Approach kerb squarely. Push foot down on tipping lever and hands down on handles and tilt wheelchair backwards onto large rear wheels.
Person: Keep head bent forward.

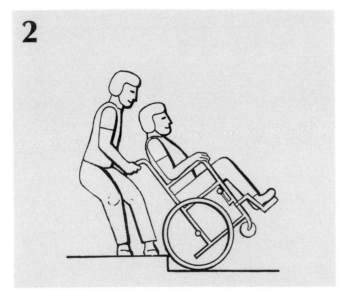

Helper: Hold chair balanced and tilted backwards and push chair forward until large rear wheels roll gently down kerb. Control speed of descent by pulling back on handles. Keep your knees bent and one foot forward of the other.

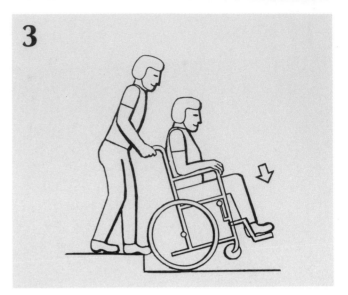

Helper: Gently lower small front wheels onto ground.

NOTE
1. *Both large rear wheels must hit the roadway together.*
2. *Person should keep head bent forward throughout this manoeuvre.*

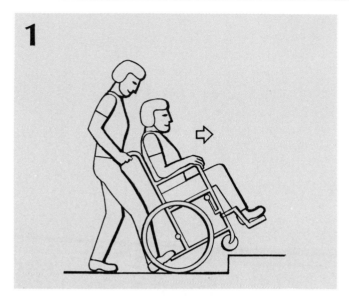

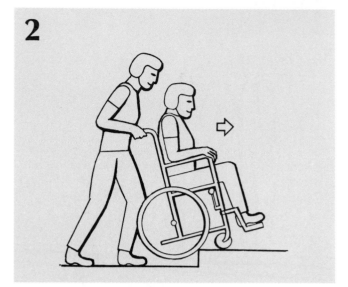

Helper: 1. Approach kerb squarely. Do not touch kerb. Push foot down on tipping lever and hands down on handles, and tilt wheelchair onto large rear wheels. Hold chair balanced and push forwards until small front wheels are up on kerb.

2. Bend knees and lift on handles. Push chair until large rear wheels are up on kerb.

NOTE
A combination of high kerb, heavy person and small helper may mean extra help is required.

REAR WHEEL DRIVE

MUCH ASSISTED
Two helpers required

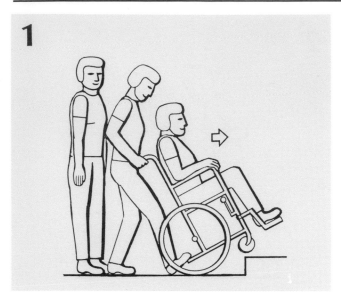

1

Helper 1: Push foot down on tipping lever and hands down on handles and tilt chair onto large rear wheels. Hold chair tilted and balanced and push it up to kerb. Lower front wheels down on kerb.
Person: Bend head forward.

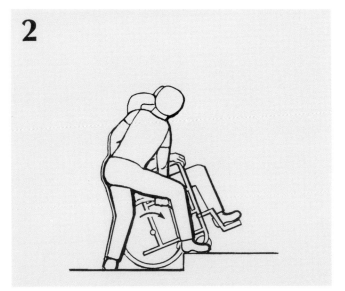

2

Helpers: Stand alongside wheelchair with front foot up on kerb and pointing in direction of movement. Back foot remains down on road and points towards wheelchair. Bend knees and put one hand on wheelchair tyre and one on handle.

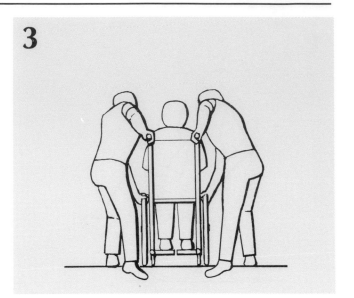

3

On command '1–2–3–push'
Helpers: Turn wheel forward and push up and forward on handle. Rock weight onto front leg and push wheelchair up onto kerb.

NOTE
Person should keep head bent forward throughout this manoeuvre.

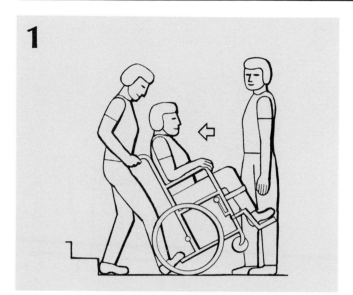

1

Helper 1: Push foot down on tipping level and hands down on handles and tilt chair on to large rear wheels.
Person: Bend head forward.

2

Helper 1: Step up stairs so that one foot is on first step and other foot is on second step. Make sure you have a secure grip and foothold. Make sure feet are parallel on step.
Helper 2: Crouch in front of wheelchair and grasp frame below arm-rests. Keep wheelchair balanced backwards throughout manoeuvre.

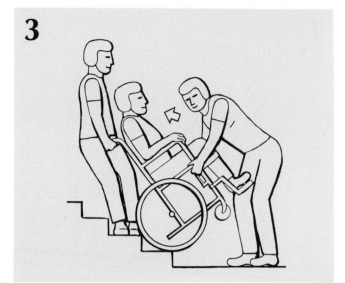

3

On command '1–2–3–up'
Helper 1: Pull on handles by thrusting weight back onto back leg, take weight of chair and pull it up one step.
Helper 2: Straighten knees and lift chair up the step.

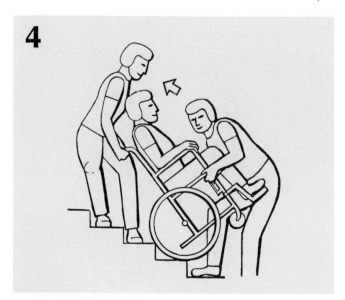

4

Helpers: Pause on new step. Repeat procedure.

NOTE
1. *Take care not to grasp any detachable or movable parts of the chair, such as detachable footplates or removable arm-rests.*
2. *The person should use calf straps (see Ch. 3) to prevent legs slipping down.*
3. *The person should keep head bent forward throughout this manoeuvre.*

175

STAIRS – DOWN FLIGHT

MUCH ASSISTED
Two helpers required

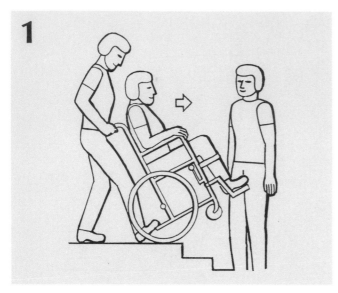

Helper 1: Push foot down on tipping lever and hands down on handles and tilt chair on to large rear wheels. Hold chair tilted and balanced and bring it to edge of stairs.
Person: Bend head forward
Helper 1: Make sure you have a secure grip and foothold. Make sure your feet are apart and parallel to step.

Helper 2: Crouch in front of wheelchair with one foot on one step and other on a step (or two) below. Upper foot pointing towards chair, lower foot parallel to step. Grasp frame below the arm-rests. Keep wheelchair balanced backwards throughout manoeuvre.

NOTE
1. Take care not to grasp any detachable or movable parts

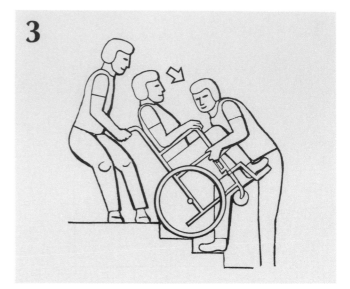

On command '1–2–3–lower'
Helper 1: Allow chair to move slowly over edge and down onto next step. Keep wheels against edge of upper step.
Control descent of chair by pulling back on handles and transfer weight from back to front leg as chair reaches lower step.
Helper 2: Steady and help brake descent of wheelchair from front by pushing against chair.

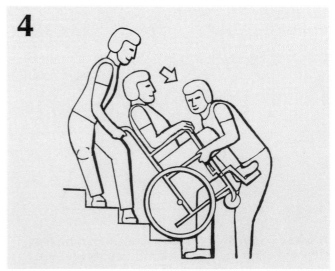

Helpers: Pause with chair on lower step. Make sure of position of feet. Repeat procedure for each step.

---

of the chair, such as detachable footplates or removable arm-rests.
2. Person must keep head forward throughout this manoeuvre.
3. The person should use calf straps (see Ch. 3) to prevent legs slipping down.

1

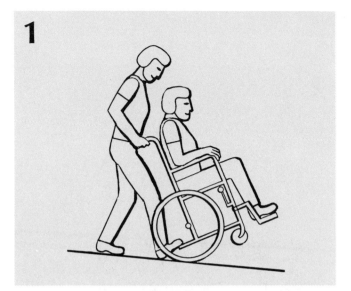

Helper: Push foot down on tipping lever and hands down on handles and tilt wheelchair onto large rear wheels. Hold chair tilted and balanced. Make sure each foot is pointed in same direction across back of chair.

2

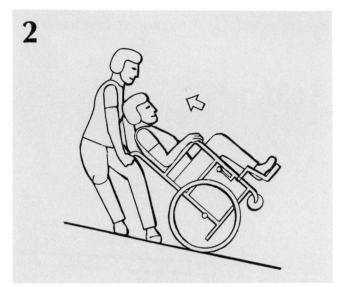

Helper: Pull on handles by thrusting weight back onto back leg and side step up slope.
Person: Bend head forward.

NOTE
1. *Person must keep head bent forward throughout the manoeuvre.*
2. *Zig-zagging up the slope will make this manoeuvre easier.*
3. *The person should use calf straps (see Ch. 3) to prevent legs slipping down.*
4. *If person is heavy or slope steep, another helper may be required.*

DOWN SLOPE
MUCH ASSISTED
One helper required

On a very steep slope it is important to control the speed of the descent of the chair. This can be done in two ways:

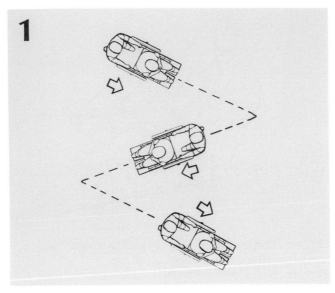

1

ZIG-ZAG
Helper: Steer the chair across face of slope several times, being careful to change direction slowly.

2

STRAIGHT
Where zig-zag isn't possible, such as on steep, narrow ramps:
Helper: Turn chair around and go down backwards, controlling descent by leaning your weight into chair. Side step backwards down slope.

The dangers in pushing wheelchairs outdoors are:

1. Breaks in the pavement surface, such as grates, holes.
2. Obstructions, such as rocks, branches, roots of trees, ruts and tussocks.
3. Loose surfaces and soft ground, such as gravel, sand or mud.

It is very easy to tip a person out of a wheelchair when it suddenly strikes even a small obstruction, especially if the small wheels are involved. Where possible, the best technique for patches of rough ground is to wheel the person on the large rear wheels only. This is more comfortable, safer and easier.

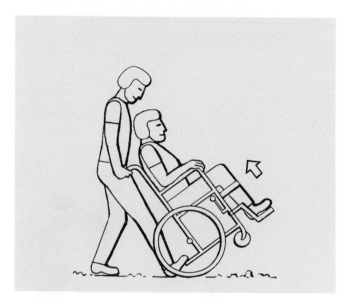

Where it is not possible to hold the chair tipped in this position, it is necessary to keep an eye out for any small obstructions and if they cannot be avoided the chair should be tipped up and over the obstruction using the tipping lever.

TO TIP CHAIR

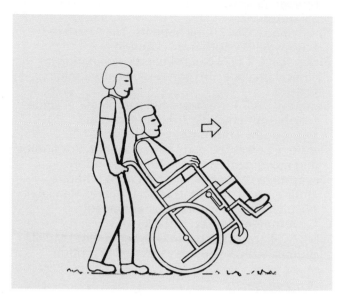

Helper: Push foot down on tipping lever and hands down on handles and tilt the chair backwards onto the large rear wheels. Hold the chair tilted and balanced backwards.

NOTE
1. *The person should use calf straps to prevent legs slipping down (see Ch. 3).*
2. *Person should keep head bent forward.*

Bibliography

Andersson G B J 1985 Permissible loads: biomechanical considerations. Ergonomics 28(1):323–326

Anonymous 1984 Lifting patients. The Chartered Society of Physiotherapy, London

Bickerstaff E R 1973 Neurological examination in clinical practice, 3rd edn. Blackwell Scientific, Oxford

Bromley I 1985 Tetraplegia and paraplegia. A guide for physiotherapists, 3rd edn. Churchill Livingstone, Edinburgh

Dardier E L 1980 The early stroke patient. Positioning and movement. Baillière Tindall, London

Department of Health Services Lifting without strain: a guide to lifting and back care. Manual of hospital lifting techniques. Tasmanian Government Printer, Hobart

Garg A, Sharma D, Chaffin D B, Schmidler J M 1983 Biomechanical stresses as related to motion trajectory of lifting. Human Factors 25(5): 527–539

Gilroy J, Holliday P L 1982 Basic neurology. Macmillan, New York

Hollis M 1981 Safer lifting for patient care. Blackwell Scientific, Oxford

Leskinen T P J, Stahlhammar H R, Kuorinka I A A, Troup J D G 1983 A dynamic analysis of spinal compression with different lifting techniques. Ergonomics 26(6): 595–604

Reeves A G 1981 Disorders of the nervous system. A primer. Year Book Medical Publishers, Chicago

Standards Association of Australia 1982 Guide to the lifting and moving of patients. Part 1: Safe manual lifting and moving of patients

Troup J D G, Leskinen T P J, Stahlhammar H R, Kuominka T A A 1983 A comparison of intra-abdominal pressure increases, hip and lumbar vertebral compression in different lifting techniques. Human Factors 25(5): 517–525